MYALGIC ENCEPHALOMYELITIS

Post-Viral Fatigue Syndrome and How to Cope With It

MYALGIC ENCEPHALOMYELITIS

Post-Viral Fatigue Syndrome and How To Cope With It

CELIA WOOKEY

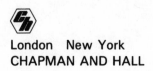

London   New York
CHAPMAN AND HALL

First published in 1986 by
Croom Helm Ltd
Reprint 1988 published by
Chapman and Hall Ltd,
11 New Fetter Lane, London EC4P 4EE

Published in the USA by
Chapman and Hall
29 West 35th Street, New York NY 10001

Reprinted 1989

© 1986 Celia Wookey

Printed in Great Britain by
Billings & Sons Limited, Worcester

ISBN 0 412 31960 8

To John

British Library Cataloguing in Publication Data

Wookey, Celia
  Myalgic encephalomyelitis: post-viral
  fatigue syndrome and how to cope with it.
  1. Encephalomyelitis   2. Myalgia
  I. Title
  616.8'3   RC370

  ISBN 0–412–31960–8

Library of Congress Cataloging in Publication Data

Myalgic encephalomyelitis.
Bibliography: p.
  Includes index.
  1. Myalgic encephalomyelitis. I. Title. [DNLM: 1. Encephalomyelitis —
physiopathology. 2. Muscular diseases — physiopathology. 3. Virus diseases —
physiopathology. WL 351 W912M]
RC370.W66 1986 616.7'3 86-13581
ISBN 0–412–31960–8 (Pbk.)

CONTENTS

FOREWORD

In May 1956 a leading article in *The Lancet* entitled 'A New Clinical Entity?' suggested that the term 'benign myalgic encephalomyelitis' might be suitable for the large number of outbreaks of infectious disease which had been reported in medical literature over the previous 20 years. From a considerable list of synonyms myalgic encephalomyelitis has been generally adopted, and is now colloquially called ME. The adjective 'benign' has been omitted since the condition, though unaccompanied by any mortality, is far from benign for those victims who suffer permanent physical incapacity as a sequel to the attack. The term 'myalgic' is certainly fully justified since an almost unique form of muscle fatiguability is the dominant clinical feature of a syndrome which may manifest itself in both epidemic and endemic forms, while 'encephalomyelitis' is likewise justified in that the condition is accompanied by varying degrees of cerebral dysfunction.

Although Coxsackie group B viruses were shown to be the aetiological agent in two outbreaks in Scotland in 1980, virological and serological investigations in most outbreaks have failed to detect any specific causative virus. Nevertheless, interest in the condition has been further aroused by three papers in the American press describing 'prolonged and atypical illnesses' following infection with Epstein-Barr (EB) virus and these illnesses are virtually identical with ME. Discussing evidence of immunological imbalance presented in these papers a leading article in *The Lancet* in May 1985 states that 'although these observations do not prove that EB virus causes chronic ill-health', nevertheless 'whatever the underlying mechanism — whether a continuing infection *per se* or an immuno-regulator disorder — the patients may be much helped by the knowledge that their persistent vague symptoms could have an organic basis'. I am in no doubt that in the very near future it will be fully established that ME is an organically determined entity and I hope that this book will aid our understanding of the condition.

Dr Melvin Ramsay

ADDITIONAL NOTE AT REPRINT

Since this book was first published there has been an unprecedented amount of publicity on ME in the media.

An impressive paper has been produced by Dr E. G. Dowsett and Dr Eleanor Bell entitled 'M.E.? A Post-Enteroviral Syndrome' (*Journal of Hospital Infection*, 1988, March issue) which makes out a very persuasive case for polio-like enteroviruses being responsible for the protean symptomatology which has baffled so many experts. They convinced me that the Coxsackie group of enteroviruses in particular are more likely to be the principal infective agents than the Epstein-Barr virus or hepatitis B.

Drs Dowsett and Bell go on to suggest that the chronic and relapsing nature of the condition can be explained by the continuing presence of the virus in tissues like peripheral muscle, the heart, central nervous system, liver, pancreas, thyroid, joints and sometimes the ovaries and the testies. They further postulate that their theory would account for the maximum age incidence (between 30 and 40), the preponderance of women, the high (25 per cent) attack rate among families and close contacts, the increased incidence among doctors and paramedical personnel, and the severity of the syndrome among so-called 'yuppies' i.e. those who have led an active life and pursued vigorous exercise particularly when the infection was latent.

They also suggest that an infection of the gut could damage the 'brush border' – the lining cells of the small intestine – and cause a malabsorption syndrome like coeliac disease. It is more than likely that the absorption of essential nutrients like amino-acids, vitamins and minerals may be impaired. Treatments for food allergy by injections or enzyme-potentiated desensitisation may flatter only to deceive and I have heard of cases where food allergy treatment actually made the patient worse. The truth of the matter may be that in a chronic relapsing and remitting condition any treatment which boosts the immune system, be it gamma-globulin injections, food allergy treatment, evening primrose oil, or nystatin and other anti-fungal agents, improves the disease for a time but improvement is not maintained.

Many patients also cannot take alcohol and are liable to drug reactions if started on treatment for depression or high blood pressure for example at too high dose because their immune system is hyperreactive. On the other hand there is some evidence that, as with alcoholism, in patients with impaired intestinal absorption and possibly subclinical liver disease, analgesic and sedative drugs are needed in higher doses.

The use of an anti-candida diet and Nystatin or other anti-fungal medication is controversial. High claims have been made for this treatment particularly in New Zealand, though the only controlled clinical trial that I know of in Dunedin, showed that Nystatin did not confer any lasting benefit. But there is abundant anecdotal evidence to support it and it may act by improving the supply of glucose to the brain. It is possible that the yeast organism capitalises on the increased need for sugar experienced by many ME sufferers.

Many ME patients, like other sufferers with immune-suppressed diseases have oral and vaginal thrush, and it can also affect the oesophagus and intestine so it is logical to try Nystatin therapy. A simple test might be to buy some Nystatin lozenges which are available over the counter and then to suck one four times a day to see if you feel any better. If they improve your illness it might be worth trying the anti-candida diet and Nystatin by mouth. It must be emphasised however that Nystatin can cause serious side-effects without the diet and should only be taken under medical supervision.

The diet is a very stringent one and it may well be asked, 'Is the treatment worse than the illness?'. According to Dr Michael Jenkins of the London Homeopathic Hospital who has most experience of treating ME patients in Britain, patients should have 2 weeks of a sugar-free, yeast-free diet, restricting carbohydrates to 80 g a day before starting Nystatin, with one sixteenth of a tsp once a day, then twice a day, working gradually up to ¼ tsp 4 times a day which may be increased to ½–1 tsp qid. If patients become depressed the answer is to double the dose, not to stop it. He thinks that much higher doses of Nystatin powder are needed for ME than the conventional tablets of 5,000 units which if taken should be increased to as much as 16 tablets a day. Fungilin (Amphotericin B) in a dose of up to 600 mg daily is a better alternative for some people. It should be remembered that if the initial improvement is not maintained it may be because the yeast organism has become resistant to the drug (particularly if used in too low a dose).

Dr Jenkins also treats his patients with Evening Primrose Oil 500 mg capsules, between 3 and 6 a day. This supplement has been shown to cut down the relapse rate if given in early cases of MS but it does not seem to have any effect in chronic sufferers.

He also uses vitamin C 1–2 g a day, Zinc 30–60 mg a day, and Magnesium and Copper supplements.

Finally, although the use of antiviral drugs like AZT and Immunovir has been disappointing, Dr Dowsett thinks that, in theory, it should be possible to develop a vaccine against those strains of Coxsackie or other enteroviruses found to cause neurological or muscle damage in man.

Celia Wookey,
February 1988

* Vitamin B12 injections, 1000 micrograms weekly, have been found to improve neurological and psychological symptoms in a small but significant trial in America, even in the absence of signs of pernicious anaemia and as this vitamin is almost entirely free of side effects, this is a treatment well worth following up.

INTRODUCTION

It has been both a challenge and a privilege to write this book, though I must admit that at first the task of writing a book about an illness of which so little is known seemed a daunting prospect. But with the help of Dr Jean Monro — to whom I am indebted for the chapter on immunology, and the patients themselves who willingly volunteered their case histories, the task has been accomplished.

As I am not an immunologist, I did not attempt the difficult feat of writing a chapter on Immunology explicable to the layman. Even so, this chapter may prove too technical for the non-scientific reader who may safely omit it without too much detriment to their understanding of the illness as a whole. The term post-viral syndrome, or post-viral fatigue syndrome, has been used by some neurologists to get the illness more readily accepted by their specialty. The reason is that it is now thought that ME is but one of a number of syndromes (the Guillain-Barré and Reye's syndromes are but two examples) that can be triggered off by a virus and it is not always possible to distinguish between them. But I think that as far as patients are concerned, this is merely a technical argument; they would much prefer to be suffering from an illness that has a definite name and a clear-cut history of epidemics. Post-viral syndrome is too vague a term to carry conviction with relatives, colleagues at work or Department of Social Security officials. It can all too easily be attributed to being work shy or sciving.

However, I hope that I have proved conclusively that ME is a disease in its own right (cf. R. T. Johnson, *Infections of the Nervous System*) primarily affecting the central nervous system, though also producing symptoms in many other parts of the body. Hopefully this book will stimulate interest in this relatively unknown disease and provoke more research into it. That is its object.

I have opened with one of the patients' stories so that readers may know at once some of the problems that those with this syndrome encounter. The case histories listed in the second part of the book are not necessarily respresentative, for many patients who were asked to contribute could not do so because they felt too ill, or their history was too long or they were fully occupied with coping with the demands of a full time job or running a home, to give the time that

1

was needed for the task. Others who had had the illness, but mildly, did not wish to be reminded of such a traumatic episode in their lives.

My thanks are due to Hilary Bright who coped with the difficult task of typing; to Dr Melvin Ramsay for valuable advice and writing the Foreword; to *World Medicine* for permission to reprint 'Anatomy of an Illness' and to William Heinemann Medical Books Ltd for permission to use the chapter on encephalomyelitis from *Sick Doctors* edited by Raymond Greene.

I would also like to thank all the people, too numerous to mention by name, who supported and encouraged me in this venture, particularly when the going was tough and the realisation of a dream seemed anything but an obtainable reality.

AUTOBIOGRAPHY

Danny Clements

On returning from a caravan holiday in September 1977, I developed a sore throat and felt rather unwell. During the following week my legs ached and I felt as though I had got flu. By the end of the second week I felt too ill to go to work and the pain in my back and legs was so unbearable I had to take to my bed.

My doctor thought I had a urinary infection, but admitted to being baffled as my temperature was below normal. The urine tests were normal, but my condition did not improve. I felt so ill, it was difficult to describe just how I felt. The symptoms were numerous and nothing gave me any relief from them. They were: headache, sore throat, stiff neck, pains especially around my shoulders, and in my legs, back, abdomen, groin and axillae. My throat was constantly sore, my eyes were sensitive to light and sound seemed magnified. I had previously enjoyed good health and was extremely fit for my 45 years. A daily workout, cycling and hiking were part of my routine and most weeks I swam 20 or so lengths during my lunch breaks. However, my wretched state continued and I felt weak and tired all the time. My doctor suggested a virus infection.

The weeks dragged on, and as I did not improve a consultant's opinion was sought; further blood tests suggested a virus infection. I was advised to pace myself. Eventually, after eight weeks, I returned to work as a draughtsman. This involves standing for long periods at my drawing board and by the end of the first week I was very fatigued and found it impossible to concentrate. I continued to go to work, but most days I crawled there and crawled to bed when I came home. After a few weeks I developed a severe pain under my right ribs; this was in addition to other symptoms of muscle pain and fatigue. I had chest and gall bladder X-rays, but everything was normal.

After six months of this illness many symptoms still persisted. I became unable to work because of severe fatigue. I was unable to walk, breathing was hard and concentrating was difficult.

Quite suddenly I developed a severe pain on the left side of my chest. It was thought I had a virus myocarditis and I was whisked

3

away to hospital. All the tests I had were once again negative and soon afterwards my doctor arranged for me to see a specialist in infectious diseases. I spent another ten days in this hospital and underwent further investigations. I was assured that I was suffering from the results of a virus infection and that the effects might last up to one or two years. Two months later I returned to work, but could only work until lunch time. About this time my wife talked to me about ME. She is a nurse and had read about the disease in a nursing journal some months before. We contacted the ME Association and I was confirmed as a possible sufferer.

A year had passed from the onset of my illness and although I had been incapacitated for most of it, as soon as I began to feel any improvement I attempted to resume my usual lifestyle.

Another year passed, very similar to the first, with a pattern of months off work when I was not able to do anything, followed by months at work crawling about. This year was followed by about four months of comparative respite, when I was able to resume hiking and swimming. 'Is it possible?' I asked myself. 'Can the nightmare have ended?' I was soon to find out — there followed a severe relapse, even worse than before.

It was suggested that I tried steroids, but the effect was devastating; the initial boost was followed by an exacerbation of symptoms. This terrible year has now passed and during that time I have not been able to work. I have had some treatment for depression and though my symptoms are less severe, I still feel awful.

I know the only treatment is to rest, but I find this very hard to do. On the days when I begin to feel any improvement at all, I find myself again involved in activity beyond my limitations. I am now well into my fourth year of illness and I find it very hard to understand being so physically incapacitated with a disease that many deny exists. My wife and I are trying to refashion our lives to fit in with these limitations. We still believe them to be temporary.

I now do the shopping and day-to-day running of the home. It poses great difficulties for me, not knowing when — or indeed if — I will ever be able to work again. We try to think positively and concentrate our efforts day by day, hardly daring to think or plan even weeks ahead. We find this is better because we avoid letting people down as cancellations can be so disappointing.

I do regret not having the Association's advice in the early stages of my illness; I think the outcome would have been different. Nevertheless we are very grateful for the Association — at least someone else understands.

I now help to run the local ME Association's 'Cheshire Group', together with some fellow sufferers. I hope by this action I can help others, as others have helped me.

Editor's Note

This history is typical.

PART ONE:

THE ILLNESS — ITS NATURE AND TREATMENT

1 HISTORY

Like glandular fever, ME exists in epidemic or sporadic form, but it is unlike glandular fever in that since there is no positive diagnostic test, the sporadic form is difficult to detect. The first recorded outbreak occurred in 1934 among the nursing and medical staff of several hospitals in Los Angeles, and surrounding districts. It was at first thought to be poliomyelitis and affected 4.5 per cent of the staff. Six months after the peak of the epidemic 55 per cent of those affected were still ill. Between 1948 and 1965, 300 sporadic cases were identified in Southern California.

Three epidemics were reported from Switzerland in 1937 in nurses and patients of a hospital at Frohburg, and one among soldiers in barracks in 1938. At this stage, the disease was regarded as an unusual illness, resembling polio and described as abortive polio. Out of 930 officers and men stationed at Erstfield, 130 were affected within twelve days; an attack rate of 14 per cent.

In the autumn of 1948, an extensive outbreak affected the town of Akureyri in Iceland (465 cases, or 6.75 per cent of the population). The initial cases appeared to have typical polio with severe paralysis, but during the next month the features of the epidemic changed to those of a new illness, hence the use of the name 'Iceland Disease' to describe it. At all ages, 8 per cent of females and 5 per cent of males were affected. The highest incidence was in the 15–19 year age group. Resident students at the high school were frequently affected; 60 per cent in one age group compared with an incidence of only 20 per cent in non-resident pupils. By 1955, when some of the patients were re-examined, only 44 per cent had fully recovered.

Further epidemics occurred in Adelaide, Australia, in 1949–50, following epidemics of poliomyelitis that summer; in a nurses' training school in Kentucky and in the community of New York State in 1950. Outbreaks also occurred within the community in Denmark (1952, 1953 and 1954) and Alaska (1954), in nurses at Bethesda, Maryland (1953) and in soldiers in Berlin (1954).

In Britain, small epidemics occurred among resident nurses at the Middlesex Hospital (London) in 1952 and the staff of a Coventry hospital in 1953. The earliest record of the major 1955 epidemic in

Great Britain came from a general practice in the village of Dalston, Cumbria. Although the first case, a workman, was reported on January 16th, the majority of cases in January and February occurred in primary school children; and the spread to adults did not occur until March and April. The epidemic continued during the summer months. Altogether 233 persons in the practice were affected, with peak case incidence in males in the 5–11 age group and in females between 20 and 29 years. Marked enlargement of lymph glands occurred in children and the glands were usually tender to touch; the glands in the neck were most commonly affected. In adults, these changes were less marked. Glandular changes had been noted previously in the New York State epidemic and the Middlesex Hospital outbreak. Involvement of the liver and spleen were frequent, with tenderness to palpation, but jaundice was rare. Subjective neurological symptoms were mentioned by 60 per cent of the patients, but objective neurological findings were present in only 20 per cent of cases, and were similar to those described in previous epidemics. About 30 per cent of the blood films showed morphological changes in the lymphocytes, but changes similar to those in glandular fever were seen in only two patients. The Paul-Bunnell tests were negative in all cases.

The vulnerability of closed communities to this disease was confirmed when the 20 children, mainly boys aged 5–15 years in Carlisle's Corporation Home, Dalston, were all affected. All cases showed glandular enlargement; some patients had only minimal symptoms but had abnormal lymphocytes in the blood films. In a number of patients the onset was insidious, with undue fatiguability, cold extremities, episodes of vertigo and aching in muscles and in the back for several weeks before the illness reached its peak. The alteration in the blood picture was found in a higher proportion of these cases than in those of acute onset. Approximately 20 per cent of the patients had recurrences of their original symptoms. In some cases, these recurrences continued for at least two years and were accompanied by persistence of the abnormal blood picture, suggesting the continuation of an organic process.

In London, the epidemic started in the early spring of 1955, when some of the clinical students at the Royal Free Hospital Medical School developed features of the illness. Then, on 13 July, a resident doctor and a ward sister were taken ill and by 27 July over 70 members of the staff were affected, causing closure of the main hospital until 5 October. Hence another name for the condition,

Royal Free Disease, was created. An initial diagnosis of glandular fever was made, but as in the Cumbrian outbreak, the Paul-Bunnell tests were negative and although abnormal lymphocytes were seen in the blood films, these were not typical of glandular fever. Neurological complications occurred much more frequently than in glandular fever and were seen in 75 per cent of the patients.

Sporadic cases continued to appear up to 24 November and altogether 292 members of the hospital staff were affected. Only 12 of the patients, who were already in hospital and inactive, developed the disease — a feature of other hospital epidemics. Rest is an important factor in the treatment of the illness and may play a preventative role in the aetiology as well. It is a well known fact that in a polio epidemic those who are worst affected are the patients who have been exercising their muscles most vigorously, and the most active muscle groups seem signalled out for attack; the same seems to hold true for ME.

Sporadic cases of the illness were seen in the community in North West London for two months before the Royal Free Hospital epidemic, and they continued to be observed for several years subsequently. In 1956 an epidemic occurred in the town of Newton-le-Willows, Lancashire (162 cases). Outbreaks have continued to occur in Britain and the USA, and also in Durban, South Africa (1955) and Iceland, again in 1955. The epidemic affecting the staff of Great Ormond Street Hospital (London) in 1970 was unusual in that there was little evidence of neurological involvement. The most recent outbreaks have occurred in Eire (1976) and Texas (1977). Sporadic cases are still frequently seen in Britain.

In 1970 the *British Medical Journal* published articles (3 January 1970, p. 11) by two psychiatrists, Drs C.P. McEvity and A.W. Beard, who considered that the epidemic was a form of mass hysteria, solely on the basis of a re-analysis of the case notes and without seeing any of the patients. Among the many objections that can be raised about their approach is their refusal to admit more than 'whatever its exact nature, the disease proved relatively benign and though a few of the affected suffered some disability for up to a year, no-one died of it.' In fact, however, they were fully aware that after 15 years there were victims of the epidemic still suffering from varying degrees of disability. Nor did they comment on evidence that sporadic cases showing a similar picture were observed in the population of North West London before and after the Royal Free outbreak (*British Medical Journal*, 7 February 1970, p. 362).

The features of hysteria that they noted were:

(1) The high attack rate in females
(2) The intensity of the malaise compared with the slight pyrexia
(3) The presence of subjective features similar to those seen in a previous epidemic of hysterical over-breathing
(4) Glove and stocking type of anaesthesia
(5) Normal findings in special investigations.

Fifteen other recorded epidemics were also reviewed and considered to be due either to hysteria on the part of the patient or to altered perception of the health of the community by the doctors concerned, so that minor everyday illnesses were seen as an epidemic.

The high attack rate in females is partly due to the increased incidence of the disease in closed communities, and the greater susceptibility among adolescents and young adults. Three epidemics have occurred among men in military barracks. Among the neurological findings in 14 nurses in the Middlesex Hospital epidemic (which the psychiatrists attributed to over-breathing), five had extensor plantar responses (a sign of central nervous system involvement) and three had ocular paralysis with double vision. Similarly, 20 per cent of the cases admitted to Lawn Road Infectious Diseases Unit in 1956 from North West London had extensor plantar responses.

There is general agreement among the clinicians who have described outbreaks of this disease that although hysterical behaviour may sometimes play a distinctive part in the manifestations of the illness, it is only part of a generalised mild encephalitic mental state in which sleep disturbances, intellectual impairment and depression of mood may feature more prominently.

In a letter to the *British Medical Journal* (1970, *1*, p. 382), Drs Richardson, Compston, Dimsdale and Ramsay pointed out that 'While a diagnosis of hysteria had been seriously considered at the time of the outbreak, the occurrence of fever in 89 per cent, of lymphadeapathy (enlarged lymph glands) in 79 per cent, of ocular palsy in 43 per cent and of facial palsy in 19 per cent rendered it quite untenable'.

Perhaps the report of the Ministry of Health for the year ended 31.12.55 Part II B provides more telling evidence against the hysteria theory, for these epidemiologists working for the ministry had no possible axe to grind. They say, 'The strange manifestations of central nervous system involvement were such that later only a diagnosis of encephalomyelitis (or polyneuritis) could be entertained. Paraesthesia, numbness and nerve pains were also frequently encountered. Cranial nerve paresis particularly ocular also occurred. Signs elicited at one examination might not be found at a subsequent one 24 hours later, but further evidence of active disease might then be apparent by the development of fresh neurological signs, of which some were fleeting, others persistent and severe. The disease had a bizarre pattern which fitted in with no known clinical entity. It bore in certain features, resemblances to encephalitis lethargica . . . Pyrexia was of a low grade and in the more severe attacks the temperature was much lower than was to be expected from the tachycardia present.'

They went on to say, 'Resident staff appeared to be more liable to attack than non-residents. Several members of the consultant staff, in the course of domiciliary consultation, in areas well removed from the hospital environment, saw persons suffering from this disease. Without doubt cases were occurring in the general population at the time, and probably also before the hospital outbreak . . . Thorough epidemiological investigations were undertaken. In February and March 1955 preliminary reports had been received of an outbreak which was occurring at that time in nurses in a hospital in Addington near Durban in South Africa. While this outbreak continued and while more detailed information was awaited, a consultant neurologist from Durban who had been associated with the Durban outbreak happened to visit this country. Arrangements were made for him to examine the cases and he confirmed the outbreak as being due to a clinical condition identical to that in Addington.'

The McEvedy and Beard article demonstrated a simple faith in the ability of mid-1950s medicine to exclude organic illness beyond doubt. Numerous letters in reply made this and other points. Perhaps the last word should rest with Dr David C. Poskanzer of the Department of Neurology, Harvard Medical School, who said in a letter to the *British Medical Journal* (16 May 1970) 'The articles of Drs C.P. McEvedy and A.W. Beard are of considerable concern because of the authors' contention that . . . Myalgic encephalomyelitis (epidemic neuromyaesthenia) is a psycho-social phenomenon related to mass hysteria or to altered medical perception in the community. Their erroneous conclusions about this illness may impair future investigations of similar outbreaks. It is apparent that the authors failed to do their homework, and demonstrated a surprising lack of information about the principles of epidemiology and of psychiatry . . . The question of mass hysteria has been considered by the authors of most papers relating to this desease and in each instance has been discarded for a number of reasons . . . It is clear that sporadic cases of this disease cannot be readily identified. It is only in the epidemic form that the distinctive epidemiological features allow characterisation. Instead of ascribing . . . myalgic encephalomyelitis to mass hysteria or psychoneurosis, may I suggest that the authors consider the possibility that all psychoneurosis is residual deficit from epidemic or sporadic cases of . . . myalgic encephalomyelitis?'

Finally, an editorial in the *British Medical Journal*, (3 June 1978, p. 1437), reporting on a symposium held in 1978 to discuss the illness, sums up the present position 'There was clear agreement that M.E. is a distinct nosological entity. Other terms used to describe the disease were rejected as unsatisfactory for various reasons: the cardinal clinical features show that the disorder is an encephalomyelitis; 'Iceland Disease' is not specific enough; and 'neuromyasthenia' suggests a relation to Myasthenia Gravis, whereas the muscle fatiguability is different as are the electrophysiological findings.' Hence, the term 'myalgic encephalomyelitis' has become the generally accepted one to describe the illness today.

2 CLINICAL PRESENTATION

ME may present in a multiplicity of different ways and it is this clinical diversity that makes diagnosis so difficult. But, broadly speaking, cases can be divided into acute and chronic. In my opinion, the diagnosis cannot be made with any degree of certainty unless the symptoms have been present for at least six months; otherwise the syndrome is almost impossible to distinguish from a state of post-viral debility following flu, glandular fever or infective hepatitis, and so on.

In the acute presentation, the initial symptom may be an attack of vomiting and diarrhoea or a sore throat associated with cough or cold. Some time later, days or weeks, the patient quite suddenly feels weak and collapses, and frequently says that he has never felt so ill in his life. He has no energy, his muscles feel like jelly and there may be severe pain in the back, legs, arms, chest or stomach. The appetite is lost and there may be vomiting and severe headache. Among other symptoms that can appear are dizziness, giddiness, pins and needles or numbness, coldness of the extremities, muscle twitching, shivering attacks, palpitations, clumsiness, difficulty in sleeping and alternating moods of depression and unnatural cheerfulness. The symptoms, particularly pain, are often worse on lying down and at night and fluctuate dramatically from day to day and from morning to evening. Some complaints such as noises in the ears or a bad taste in the mouth are so bizarre that the patient or his doctor or both may think they must be psychological.

On medical examination, there is little unusual to find. Most patients have a slight fever (rarely exceeding 100°F, 37.8°C), but sometimes there is hypothermia to a temperature as low as 95°, a rapid pulse and a 'ghastly' pallor often associated with a low blood pressure. Though the muscles are weak, there may be no wasting, but muscle-twitching (fasciculation) can be an important diagnostic sign. Sometimes the doctor may be able to detect swelling of the lymph nodes or the liver, or conjunctivitis, stiffness of the neck, tenderness of muscles, patches of numbness or flickering of the eyes (nystagmus).

Some patients recover within a few weeks or months, but in others the illness drags on. At this stage there are three features found in almost every case: patients tire easily, their symptoms vary from day to day and their emotional state also fluctuates. Usually the tiredness increases as the day wears on; many patients are completely exhausted by the afternoon. The illness has psychological effects too; depression, insomnia, an inability to concentrate, loss of memory, nightmares and mood swings. Usually there is slow recovery over a period of months or even years, but there may be relapses brought on by intercurrent infection, over-exertion or a too-early return to work.

This is a typical ME presentation, but many cases are atypical and can be confused with a variety of other illnesses, such as prolapsed intervertebral disc, a heart attack, an acute abdominal emergency, or as a personality disorder in which irritability and paranoia may be the predominant features. This will be discussed more fully in a later chapter, and the case histories of various patients at the end of this book will illustrate the misdiagnoses that can so easily be made. It is sufficient to say here that the diagnosis should be considered in any long-term clinical illness with atypical features, and confirmatory evidence may be found if the patient is asked if any relative or friend was ill at the same time, even if their symptoms were different.

I have found that in chronic cases with a history dating back over many years, the simplest method of making the diagnosis (in the absence of a specific diagnostic test) is to ask patients to fill in a questionnaire. The salient features are illustrated in Figure 2.1. The important symptoms from the diagnostic point of view are listed in column one. They are: headache; pain (aching) in the back of the neck; muscle pain in the back, arms or legs; sore eyes; sensitivity to light; excessive fatigue; physical weakness; heavy feeling of the legs; difficulty in standing; pins and needles in the arms or legs; difficulty in carrying heavy weights or lifting arms above head; numbness; clumsiness; giddiness/dizziness; muscle twitching; shivering attacks; loss of appetite; nausea; looking pale or grey; puffiness under the eyes; cold hands and feet; loss of memory; loss of concentration; insomnia; depression and difficulty in passing water. When the questionnaire was first devised, the symptom of 'feeling awful' was included in the first column, but this was subsequently deleted on the grounds that it was too non-specific, although it was surprising how many patients volunteered the information that they had never felt so awful in their lives.

In an initial pilot study of the use of this questionnaire, 322 forms were returned and on the basis of the information received 258 of these were diagnosed as probable ME sufferers. This was in response to a radio broadcast on ME in 'Woman's Hour', so the preponderance of women patients is not as great as the statistics would seem to suggest. Nevertheless, some useful information was obtained.

The total number of patients accepted as ME sufferers was 258 with an age range of 8 – 74 years. The number of men was 42 and women 216. The duration of illness was from 1 to 44 years. Twenty four per cent had had the illness from 1 to 2 years; 29 per cent 3 to 10 years; 24 per cent 11 to 20 years and 15 per cent 21 to 44 years. Only 5 per cent claimed to be cured or had no history of relapses, while 3 per cent could not give any date of onset. In the 61 persons with a 1 to 2-year history, 57 per cent claimed to be improving; 36 per cent remained the same and only 6 per cent thought they were getting worse. But of the 76 persons who had had the illness from 3 to 10 years, 21 per cent claimed to be improving, 46 per cent remained the same and 27 per cent were getting worse. For the 52 persons who had had the illness for 11 to 20 years, the figures were: 25 per cent improving; 38 per cent remaining the same and 27 per cent getting worse. In the 20 to 44 year group of 38 patients: 15 per cent claimed to be improving; 40 per cent remained the same and 38 per cent said they were getting worse.

In 31 per cent of patients there was a sudden onset of symptoms, while in 61 per cent the onset was more gradual. Previous health was good in 75 per cent, but it is interesting to note that no less than 52 per cent gave a family history of allergy. Other members of the family were affected in 17 per cent and 51 per cent were left with permanent muscle weakness. The symptoms varied from day to day in 87 per cent of patients and during the day in 77 per cent. Forty one per cent claimed to be worse in the morning, 25 per cent at night and 22 per cent said it varied. A list of the percentage of sufferers complaining of the most common symptoms is shown in Table 2.1

Thus it can be seen that no patient should be without hope of possible improvement, though the longer he has had the illness the worse the prognosis. However, in multiple sclerosis, the relapse rate decreases with years, and those who have had the illness longest will automatically have fewer relapses and the same may be true of ME. It appears that rest at the outset can minimise the severity of the illness, while excessive physiotherapy or treating the patient as psychological can make it worse. Many patients report long years free of relapses and if the patient lives within his limitations, he can

Figure 2.1: Myalgic Encephalomyelitis Questionnaire

Please complete and return to: Mrs Pam Searles,
"The Moss"
Third Avenue,
Stanford-le-Hope, Essex.

As only a very limited number of volunteers are dealing with this, it may be some months before analysis and answers can be returned. Please enclose stamps for replies.

Name

Address   Date of onset

Telephone No.   Place of onset

Date of Birth   Activity at time of onset

Mr/Mrs/Miss   Connection with
                                                                  similar cases

Occupation
                                                                  Connection with
Name and address of   children
   your doctor

Please indicate by a tick if you have experienced any of the following symptoms since you became ill:

Column 1

(1)	Headache	(14)	Giddiness-dizziness
(2)	Pain in back of neck	(15)	Muscle twitching
(3)	Muscle pain in back, arms or legs	(16)	Shivering attacks
(4)	Sore eyes	(17)	Loss of appetite
(5)	Sensitivity to light	(18)	Nausea
(6)	Excessive fatigue	(19)	Looking pale or 'grey'
(7)	Physical weakness	(20)	Cold hands and feet
(8)	Legs feeling heavy	(21)	Loss of memory
(9)	Difficulty in standing	(22)	Loss of concentration
(10)	Pins and needles in arms or legs	(23)	Insomnia
(11)	Difficulty in carrying heavy weights or lifting arms above head	(24)	Depression
		(25)	Difficulty in passing water
		(26)	Puffiness of eyes[a]
(12)	Numbness	(27)	Spontaneous bruising[a]
(13)	Clumsiness		

Column 2

(1)	Stiffness of neck	(6)	Palpitations
(2)	Pain in abdomen	(7)	Abdominal distention
(3)	Fainting	(8)	Vaginal discharge
(4)	Vomiting	(9)	Excessive flatulence
(5)	Abnormal bowel movements	(10)	Blurred vision

Column 3

(1) Sore throat
(2) Pain in chest
(3) Tremor
(4) Noises in ears
(5) Sensitivity to noise
(6) 'Indigestion'

(7) Frequent crying
(8) Nightmares
(9) Shortness of breath
(10) Hoarseness
(11) Speech difficulties

Column 4

(1) 'Cold in head'
(2) Raised temperature
(3) Rash or irritation of skin
(4) Painful joints
(5) Earache
(6) Deafness
(7) Seeing double
(8) Cough

(9) Frequency in passing water
(10) Dry mouth
(11) Flushing
(12) Increased thirst
(13) Sweating unduly
(14) Panic feelings
(15) Guilt feelings
(16) Bad taste in mouth

Have your symptoms varied from day to day? Or during the day?
Are they worse in morning/afternoon/at night?
Are they worse lying down?
Did you become ill suddenly/gradually?
Was your health previously good?
Were any other members of your family affected?
Have you any family history of allergy, e.g. hay fever, asthma, eczema, skin rashes, reactions to drugs or foods?
Do you feel ill or irritable when hungry or if exercise has tired you out?
Are you improving/getting worse/about the same?
Do you have any permanent muscle weakness, such as difficulty in standing, lifting arms above the head or carrying heavy weights?
Do climatic conditions, e.g. sunlight, have any effect on your symptoms?
Have you had any blood or electrical tests or other investigations, e.g. lumbar puncture?
If so, did they show anything?
What diagnosis, if any, have you been given?
What treatment, if any, are you having?
Would you be prepared, if selected, to go to a hospital and possibly be admitted for a short time for tests which will further research into this illness but not necessarily result in any new treatment for you?
Will you give your permission for us to contact your doctor if necessary?

Space for comments

Have you discovered any particular factor, e.g. standing around, that seems to make your symptoms worse?

Note:[a] These were later additions to the original list of symptoms which seemed to be useful diagnostically lessen the degree to which the illness restricts his life.

It was interesting to find that women are much more prone to suffer from this illness than men, though as explained previously this sample was biased. Medical and paramedical personnel were well represented though they comprised only 12 per cent of the total. It did appear that there was a greater tendency for women patients to suffer also from gynaecological disorders and an unexpected finding was the high percentage of patients (58 per cent) reporting painful joints.

Table 2.1: Questionnaire Questions

(1)	Excessive fatigue	90%
(2)	'Feeling awful'	89%
(3)	Muscle pain in back, arms or legs	83%
(4)	Loss of concentration	80%
(5)	Headache	79%
(6)	Physical weakness	78%
(7)	Looking pale or grey	75%
(8)	Pain in the back of neck	75%
(9)	Giddiness/dizziness	71%
(10)	Cold hands and feet	69%
(11)	Legs feeling heavy	66%
(12)	Depression	66%
(13)	Pins and needles in arms or legs	65%
(14)	Clumsiness	65%
(15)	Muscle twitching	64%
(16)	Difficulty in carrying heavy weights,or lifting arms above head.	64%
(17)	Stiffness of neck	62%
(18)	Sensitivity to light	60%
(19)	Painful joints	58%
(20)	Nausea	57%
(21)	Sensitivity to noise	57%
(22)	Difficulty in standing	56%
(23)	Numbness	54%
(24)	Sore eyes	53%
(25)	Shivering attacks	50%
(26)	Insomnia	49%
(27)	Palpitations	49%
(28)	Panic feelings	48%
(29)	Pain in abdomen	47%
(30)	'Indigestion'	46%
(31)	Blurred vision	46%
(32)	Pain in chest	45%
(33)	Sore throat	44%
(34)	Abdominal distention	43%
(35)	Noises in ears	43%
(36)	Dry mouth	42%
(37)	Sweating unduly	42%
(38)	Frequency in passing water	42%
(39)	Bad taste in mouth	42%

(40) Constipation 42%
(41) Shortness of breath 41%
(42) 'Cold in the head' 41%
(43) Loss of memory 40%
(44) Loss of appetite 39%
(45) Fainting 36%
(46) Increased thirst 34%
(47) Flushing 33%
(48) Diarrhoea 32%
(49) Frequent crying 32%
(50) Guilt feelings 29%
(51) Vaginal discharge (216 questionnaires) 29%
(52) Raised temperature 28%
(53) Nightmares 27%
(54) Cough 25%
(55) Earache 25%
(56) Vomiting 24%
(57) Rash 24%
(58) Seeing double 22%
(59) Tremor 17%
(60) Deafness 15%
(61) Difficulty in passing water 12%

3   IMMUNOLOGY

Jean Monro
Director of Allergy and Environmental Medicine,
Florence Nightingale Hospital, London

What is Immunology?

Immunology is the science of the body's defence against infection by micro-organisms and other foreign substances. The system therefore is distributed throughout the body. In order to be able to attack foreign substances but leave the body's own varied cells unharmed, there are very specific coding systems, enabling the defence mechanism to recognise self and react specifically to infecting agents. We rarely suffer twice from diseases such as measles, and this ability to remember previous exposures is a basic function of the system.

Contact with a foreign substance (called an antigen, i.e. something which provokes the generation of antibodies) leads to the creation of antibodies (anti-foreign bodies) by the white blood cells, at first slowly, over two or three days. This is the primary response. The second exposure to the same antigen gives a much faster response, called the secondary response, due to the memory effect. Antibodies dispose of the foreign agent either by producing chemicals which react directly with the invader, or by binding themselves to the invading substances and so making them inert. Alternatively they can attract other white cells which ingest the invader. The antibody can usually be saved for future use by separation.

Antibodies circulate in the body as proteins called immunoglobulins, of which there are five main types; IgA, IgD, IgE, IgM, and IgG. Each type has a particular function. IgA is found chiefly in body secretions; IgD is thought to control the activity of other cells; IgE protects the mucous surfaces of the body; IgM is associated with blood groups and related reactions and IgG is the chief immunoglobulin synthesised against invaders. Any deficiency of these immunoglobulins will result in an illness called immunodeficiency, but an excess can cause hypersensitivity.

The fundamental immune responses are the production of the antibody and its release into the blood and other body fluids, and the production of lymphocytes and macrophages. Lymphocytes are white blood cells which are made in bone marrow. Under the microscope they look like very simple cells which have a nucleus surrounded by cytoplasm. They all look very similar in their adult form, but functionally they differ because each has a memory imprinted on it by having matured in different regions of the body. Those which are matured in lymphoid tissue become B cells. Those which mature in the body's thymus gland become T lymphocytes. The B cells are concerned with the production of free immuno-globulins and the T lymphocytes are responsible for cellular immunity. The lymphocytes can only be distinguished by their function, but they have on their surfaces various markers which can be used to identify them in the laboratory. Macrophages act with lymphocytes to destroy antigens. Sometimes they simply ingest the microbes but at other times they incorporate them into their surface membranes and present them to the lymphocytes for destruction. Genetic factors influence the immune response and feedback mechanisms which operate to limit antibody production. Once an infection is curbed the production of antibodies is limited until the body has a further exposure.

Yet another means by which the invader can be destroyed is by the activation of the complement system, freely circulating chemicals which can make chemical dissolutions of the membranes of foreign cells. Enzymes are released in a sequence from this system, through the activation of a cascade of components from complement factors from one to nine.

To prevent infection, the body has means of protecting itself from the entry of the infecting agents. The skin is impermeable to most infectious agents. Fatty acids in the sweat and sebaceous secretions protect locally, and mucus secreted by membranes acts as a protective barrier and contains antibodies. Once in the body, however, the two main defensive operations are to dissolve the bactericidal enzymes and to ingest the bacteria, in which the interplay of complement, antibody and phagocytic cells is a tripartite defence mechanism. Deficiency in any one of these factors reduces one's resistance to repeated infections, especially bacterial infections. Deficiency of T-cell lymphocytes results in impaired ability to cope with viral infections in particular. Unfortunately, viral infections themselves often cause a deficiency of T cells, leading to recurrences of the viral infection.

Once an individual has been in contact with the antigen, and its policing system can recognise the foreign agent, further contact with the antigen leads to boosting of the immune response. If the reaction is excessive it can actually lead to tissue damage, which is known as hypersensitivity. This normal reaction of the body has been grouped into five types,

(1) In type 1 hypersensitivity, antigen and antibody react on the surface of the cells called mast cells or circulating basophils, and these cells degranulate releasing from granules in their cytoplasm a number of proteins which can have vascular effects, including shock.

(2) In type 2 hypersensitivity, antibodies attach themselves to antigens which are on the cells surfaces causing other cells to be attracted to the area to ingest the attacked cell. These cells are also attacked by complement which degrades the surface of the attacked cell.

(3) Type 3 hypersensitivity occurs when antibody and antigen are circulating in a complex, and can cause platelets, which are tiny particles in the blood, to aggregate. These aggregations may be deposited in small blood vessels and cause local reactions.

(4) In type 4 hypersensitivity, antigen reacts with primed T cells and soluble mediators (lymphokines) are released. If the antigen is not killed completely, then continuing provocation of the delayed hypersensitivity results in the formation of a tissue called a granuloma.

(5) In type 5 hypersensitivity, the antibody reacts with some cell surface components which may stimulate rather than destroy the cell. This review of immunity is of importance in the understanding of disease processes due to infecting agents.

ME: A Review of Epidemics

ME is an inflammatory disease whose cause is unknown. However, the feature which leads us to assume that it must be infectious in origin is that it occurs in epidemic form. There is no other means by which an epidemic can occur unless it be exposure to a toxin, but the review of the features of the epidemics excludes toxic factors as being responsible because there has been no constant exposure to such agents. The features of the epidemics are important because they may lead to an understanding of what the provocative agents are.

The first outbreak reported was in Los Angeles in 1934, where it was thought that there was an unusual form of poliomyelitis occurring in the hospital and surrounding districts. It was unusual because it had a relatively high attack rate with a low mortality rate and a low paralytic rate. There was a high incidence in adults. One important epidemic attacked 198 members of the medical and nursing staff of Los Angeles County General Hospital. The initial symptoms were malaise, headache, fever, double vision, constipation, retention of urine and muscular weakness. There was some mental disturbance with loss of concentration, sensory changes with muscle pain and tenderness and hypersensitivity of the skin. Observers concluded that the cause of the epidemic was a disease spread by direct personal contact, not by contamination of the hospital milk or food supply.

A second outbreak occurred in 1937 when 130 soldiers stationed at Erstfield, Switzerland became affected by an illness in which sweating, fever, oversensitive skin and muscle pains occurred, sometimes with weakness. Fortunately, the attack seemed to have no permanent effects. Another outbreak of infection occurred at the Hospital for St Gall in Frohburg, Switzerland, in September 1937. Fourteen people became ill with headache, weakness of the muscles and marked fatigue; a prolonged convalescence was required for these patients. In 1939 at Degershein, again in Switzerland, 800 officers and men arrived in September and during September and October there were 73 cases of patients with a flu-like illness, headache and muscle weakness, and in some cases a long period of convalescence was required.

In Iceland in September 1948 a case of poliomyelitis was reported. Thereafter the number of cases quickly grew, and 6 per cent of the population of three towns was affected. Nearly 1000 cases were reported, many of them children in a high school with the boarders being affected much more commonly than the day pupils. The characteristics were: a low fever; muscle tenderness; lassitude; muscle weakness and neuritis affecting the shoulder girdle and the legs. Virus studies then failed to involve poliomyelitis, Coxsackie or other encephalitic viruses. Seven years later, 39 of the patients who were afffected in the worst outbreak were examined by a neurologist; only 25 per cent had completely recovered. At about the same time in Iceland there was an epidemic of poliomyelitis which spread round the coast.This was distinguished from the encephalomyelitis outbreak by a finding of antibodies to poliomyelitis virus in those who had the classic polio condition, whereas there was no such raised antibody in the children in the areas affected by the encephalomyelitis condition.

There was an epidemic of poliomyelitis in Adelaide, Australia, in May 1949. In August, cases of ME began to appear and continued to be seen until 1951, by which time 800 patients had been admitted to the Infectious Diseases Hospital. Patients with poliomyelitis had abnormal cerebrospinal fluid, which circulates round the brain and spinal cord. Those with encephalomyelitis did not. Furthermore, those patients who had the encephalomyelitis also had chest infections, muscle weakness and a relapsing condition which recurred the following year. Investigations for viruses were negative, but a transmissable agent was identified, because a tissue injected into monkeys from two patients caused red spots to develop along the course of the sciatic nerve with damage to the nerve fibres. Also, in the spinal cord and brain of the monkeys vascular changes were seen.

There was an epidemic in New York State in 1950 when poliomyelitis occurred simultaneously. At the time 33 patients with myalgic encephalomyelitis were described. In an epidemic in Rockville, USA, paracolon organisms were found to have been involved in the precipitation of the epidemic. In 1955 in Cumbria, 233 cases were recorded with febrile illness, enlarged lymph glands and a large number of lymphocytes present in the blood stream. Nervous system changes occurred in about 60 per cent of the patients. Unfortunately virus studies performed were negative. By July 1955 the condition had spread to County Durham and a similar outbreak occurred in a boy's school at Sedbergh in Yorkshire. Between April 1955 and September 1957, 53 patients were admitted to the infectious diseases department of the Royal Free Hospital suffering from ME. Headache, muscle weakness, pain and malaise occurred in most of the patients; many of them were hospital staff. Biological and serological investigations were negative, but in all of these cases there was a lowering in the level of white cells (a leucopenia,which is characteristic of a virus infection).

A further epidemic in London occurred in North Finchley between 1964 and 1967, in which abnormal muscular fatigue was the constant feature. Yet another occurred at the Hospital for Sick Children, Great Ormond Street, between August 1970 and January

1971, in which 145 cases were observed amongst the nurses in particular. Again, virological investigations were negative. Coxsackie B1 virus was isolated from a throat swab from one patient in the outbreak, adenovirus type 3 from a throat and rectal swab of another patient and an adenovirus type 5 from the throat of a third patient was also found. A few of these patients had more antibodies to Coxsackie B5. Serum immunoglobulins were normal.

In an outbreak in South West Ireland in September 1976, fatigue, pallor, headache, dizziness, nausea and vomiting occurred in 15 patients, some of whom were thought to have myalgic encephalomyelitis. In the summer of 1975, an extensive epidemic of disease which was identified as being due to echovirus type 19 occurred in the West Midlands. These patients had an aseptic meningitis and the virus was isolated in a major portion of the patients (70 per cent). The patients mainly had fever, pain in the muscles (particularly around the chest), headache and vomiting. In 1977 in Dallas, USA, a further epidemic occurred; serological tests on 28 patients were negative. In 1980 at a girl's school in Southampton, 45 girls developed headache, vomiting and weakness; no pathogens or viruses were found. There was a further report between January 1980 and June 1981 of an outbreak in Ayrshire; many of the affected patients were found to have raised antibody titres to group B Coxsackie viruses. Of a group of 20 patients whose serum was examined, 15 had raised antibody titres.

This review of the reported epidemics gives us many clues as to the cause of the problem, and practically all the patients in each outbreak have been in fairly close communities. They were either hospital staff, inmates of schools or forces personnel. This indicates that the agent responsible must be contagious. Despite searches for viruses, there have not been constant findings of raised antibody titres to any particular virus, though in some outbreaks high levels of antibodies to Coxsackie B viruses have been found. Viral infections are extremely common, with perhaps half a dozen respiratory virus infections each year for many individuals. In many of the outbreaks there has been a definite association with parallel incidence of poliomyelitis. After an infection occurs, the virus may be dealt with promptly by the immunological mechanisms that have been described, resulting in complete elimination of the virus. If it becomes persistent due to some sort of immunological shortfall, the virus will live within cell bodies and a recrudescence of symptoms may occur if the individual is under concurrent immunological stress from another infection or other constitutional factors, such as loss of sleep, emotional stress and so on. Hence the recurring nature of the disease.

The fact that myalgic encephalomyelitis occurs in epidemics indicates that an infective agent is responsible. In any local outbreak many people may be contaminated, but only if the infection causes overt disease do we recognise the infection. Many people will have a sub-clinical infection which can be converted into clinical infection by changing circumstances.

Clinical Features: Natural History of ME and Transmission

Some people who develop ME recover completely from the acute infection, while in others the disease becomes latent with recurrent relapses. The disease may be transferred by droplets or by direct contact, occasionally by fomites, which are household items that are in contact with the patient, such as bedding, books and other personal possessions and equipment. Sometimes the soil can be contaminated. In general, however, with virus diseases the transmission is both by infected patients and by carriers, who can be symptomless or convalescent, or even those incubating the disease.

The patients usually start by having a respiratory infection and often the lymph nodes are enlarged. Often there has been no detectable bacterial cause and the presence of a virus has therefore been suggested. Viruses do not reproduce themselves. They enter host cells and are replicated there. The virus nucleic acid enters the host cell and takes control of its mechanisms for nucleic acid and protein synthesis, diverting them to the production of virus components. Viruses are therefore human parasites, though some have other animal species as their principal host. Those viruses which cause respiratory tract infections are predominantly transferred by droplet infection, but some called entero-viruses, such as poliomyelitis are acquired by ingestion. Viruses generally invade and multiply in the cells around their port of entry into the host's body, but there is lymphatic and blood stream spread from the site of primary infection to other parts of the body. Often a latent infection occurs and recurrent signs of this can be seen, for example, in the recurrent herpes cold sores on the lips.

A human host, once it encounters a virus, can have an acute infection and dispose of the virus completely, but once the virus is established the host's ability to survive and recover from the infection depends on how much damage the virus can do to the cells and the particular functions of those cells that are susceptible to it. In people who have polio, some of the cells are destroyed and paralysis can result. The virus can, however, be destroyed completely, leaving only the sequelae of the initial onslaught. In virus diseases cell-mediated immunity is one of the most important components of acquired resistance.

Laboratory Diagnostic Tests

The laboratory diagnosis of virus infections requires a clinical understanding of how the disease occurs and the pattern it shows in its natural history. Ordinary light microscopy is very rarely useful in virological diagnosis. Electron microscopy can be far more informative but electron microscopes are expensive and relatively rare. The presence of a virus need not mean that it has been responsible for a particular illness. Serological testing to find raised antibody levels is a useful method, but it has to be repeated to prove that the condition is current rather than long-standing. If there is a rise in antibody concentration over a period, it is likely that there is current infection.

Virus Classification

A very brief description of virus groups may help. The classification is based on the recognition of different structures as well as the mode of transmission and other features of the diseases they cause. Enteroviruses are intestinal. Of the enteroviruses, polio virus and Coxsackie virus are amongst the most important ones. Polio viruses are isolated in human tissue and are recoverable from throat swabs during the first few days of the illness; antibodies appear in the blood following infection and give lasting immunity. People can be immunised against this type of virus. Coxsackie viruses were first isolated in Coxsackie, USA. They are divided into two groups, A and B, and cause aseptic meningitis, epidemic myalgia, Bornholms disease (in which there is muscular pain around the chest wall, fever with rashes, and an acute sore throat) hand, foot and mouth disease, and sometimes myocarditis, an inflammation of the heart muscle.

The diagnostic procedures that are used are similar to those used for poliomyelitis.

Echoviruses (Enteric Cytopathogenic Human Orphan viruses) are present in human faeces. Some of the 30 or so types can cause aseptic meningitis and a febrile illness, with or without rashes, diarrhoea and respiratory tract infections. Other types of viruses include: a rhinovirus, responsible for common colds; reoviruses which are Respiratory Enteric Orphan viruses, myxoviruses which include influenza viruses, mumps, measles; para-influenza viruses; respiratory syncytial virus; rabies viruses; arboviruses; rubella virus; adenoviruses; herpes viruses; pox and hepatitis viruses. Their characteristics differ according to the conditions they cause and their pathological features.

Two major groups of viruses have been linked with myalgic encephalomyelitis. One is the Coxsackie group and the other poliomyelitis, though no absolute relationship between virus and disease has been confirmed.

Management

As with any other acute virus disease, once the acute stage of ME is over, there may be no further problem. However, if the mechanism of the immunity does not entirely eliminate the virus, then the infection becomes chronic. Interferon may be generated by unrelated viruses and different strains of the same virus. This interferon is a protein of low molecular weight, which when injected into a cell susceptible to a virus, can interfere with virus replication, apparently by preventing synthesis of the viral nucleic acid. Hence treatment is possible with interferon, but this is not yet generally available. Treatment of viral conditions will depend on augmenting the host's response, either with vaccines given to invoke antibody production before the virus is met, or by increasing the general constitutional resistance to infection by ensuring that the individual is in a good nutritional state. These two methods are preventative, but once the infection has occurred there are very few satisfactory methods. Management must therefore be supportive in an acute phase, with general nursing care and attention to diet and rest. Later, however, in exacerbations of the condition the only recommendations that have been consistently offered are to avoid exercise or tiring the muscles which are particularly painful.

What other management methods are available to mitigate symptoms? A major possibility is to consider that the immune system, having been unsettled by the virus onslaught, may be reacting to other agents. This has been demonstrated as being a causative factor in many patients. The constant effect of any virus infection is to cause a depletion of some of the white cells, called the neutrophil polymorphs. This is almost a hallmark of virus infections, in that there is a neutropenia. The T-cell lymphocytes are the ones that are particularly called upon to kill cells which have been invaded by bacteria, and in chronic diseases it has been demonstrated that there is an imbalance between the numbers of T lymphocytes compared with the B lymphocytes.

Studies have shown that if the T-cell levels are depleted considerably, the body will be hypersensitive and hyper-reactive to a wide range of substances, many of which are not normally disease-causing, but which may be required for nutritional or other purposes. In environmental care units, where the air is filtered and the food offered is as pure as possible (i.e. grown without chemical fertilizers, fungicides or insecticides), patients with post-viral syndromes have been found to have low levels of T lymphocytes; on treatment with immunotherapy based on the use of a technique known as the provocation/neutralisation method, patients have been able to overcome the over-reactivity to normal substances in their everyday lives and gradually the T-cell populations have risen to a more normal level. With this restoration of normality to the blood picture, many of the chronic symptoms of the post-viral syndromes have been cleared. This technique is not yet widely accepted and is not available to all sufferers, but it is an area in which further research is warranted.

The state of instability which follows some virus infections can be due to the lack of a feedback mechanism protecting the body from hypersensitivity and over-reactivity, and may be regarded as a form of allergy. The term allergy was first used by the German pathologist, Peter von Pirquet in 1906. The term means 'altered in reaction' and comes from the Greek allos (altered) and ergon (reaction). Altered reactivity is what is being experienced by many people who have recurrent virus infections, as they are unable to use their defence mechanisms to throw off the infection completely. One type of reaction is known as atopy, which means out of place. This type of reaction is the acute form of reaction with which people are familiar; that is asthma, eczema and hay fever. However, in post-viral syndromes the clinical picture is of a polysymptomatic complaint with wide-ranging symptoms; such environmental illness can be maintained by chronic exposure to low doses of multiple substances. Classic allergy mechanisms are not necessarily involved, but other dysfunctions of the immune system have been implicated. In such a person who is unstable with regard to environmental agents, this concept of environmental sensitivity is the basis of the new science of environmental medicine.

Many patients have described hypersensitivity to foods, chemicals and inhalants after a virus infection, and the old method of management of these patients is somewhat limited. There are many ways in which allergies can affect the body: asthma, eczema, rhinitis, urticaria, hay fever and migraine are well-known. We are now recognising their responsibility in colitis, arthropathies, conditions of extreme fatigue, recurrent cystitis and other conditions in which multiple symptoms can occur. The reason why so many systems can be involved is that the cells responsible for allergies are widely distributed in the blood and tissues.

People who have inhalant allergies from problems such as dust and pollen also react to some foods or chemicals in their environment. These people can be treated by avoidance of exposure to the offending substances or by minimising exposure by varying the diet so that one does not repeat the same foods too frequently. Foods can be divided into food families: for instance the apple family, which is derived from the rose family. Relatives of the apple are pear, strawberry, raspberry, blackberry, rosehip, quince and so on. This extensive family can have common antigens, that is there may be something inherent in all of them which can cause reactions in an individual who is sensitive to one of them. Another example is wheat, which is in the graminacae family. Other relatives of this family include millet, rice, maize, oats, barley, rye, sugar cane, bamboo shoots. The derivatives of these are important and include the derivatives of corn, such as glucose syrup (for which synonyms are corn sugar, dextrose, invert sugar, confectioner's sugar) and corn oil, which appears not only under that name but also in mixtures of vegetable oils and most margarines. There are cross-reactions between the members of the grain family, so that someone reacting to wheat will probably react to maize and oats; this reaction will be difficult to discern if the person is eating an ordinary mixed diet. Often patients need guidance on varying their diets and many menus and diet sheets have been devised to show how to vary the exposure to food families and thus minimise the amount of potential allergen taken — 'a diversified rotational diet'.

It is possible to test peoples' sensitivities by having a blood test for a number of antigens. For example, one can test for a wide range of foods and inhalants using tests which will discover the amount of antibody against any particular food or antigen, i.e. foreign substance. Reliable methods for this type of detection are, however, few. They entail variations of the process below:

Food is added to the patient's serum and the resulting complex is fixed either to the solid food or to a paper disc. Any free food is washed away, as is serum which has not been attached to the food. The complex can be measured either using a fluorescent tag or a radioactive substance which will attach to human particles. The amount of fluorescence can be gauged by an experienced observer and an indication given of whether a particular antibody is present, or a Geiger counter can be used to ascertain how much reactivity there is in the sample. These methods are scientific. They are not the only ones available.

Apart from blood tests, there are skin tests which can be used to help to make a diagnosis. Routine skin tests (prick tests) are not generally suitable for most food allergy identification, though they are useful to discover inhaled allergies, being qualitative not quantitative.

A further method called the provocation/neutralisation method is available for testing for allergies. This entails injecting a small quantity of food or other substance just under the skin. The resulting wheal is measured immediately, and again after ten minutes. If there has been any enlargement of the wheal then the patient is considered to be sensitive to that item because it has caused disruption of cells and exudation of histamine, with the resulting summoning of tissue fluid to that area and an enlargement of the wheal. The patient will then have a weaker dilution of the same item injected and this will cause a lesser reaction. The exact concentration that does not provoke a symptom or increase the size of the wheal is used in treatment and, taken regularly, this neutralising technique can, in a short period, desensitise some individuals to these foods. In others, a more prolonged treatment is required before the patient will be able to live without symptoms from that food.

Because allergies are not static but dynamic, depending upon a patients' exposure and state of health, there are sometimes fluctuations in a patient's condition and this has led to difficulties in treatment and diagnosis in the past. The method of provocation/neutralisation is very finely tuned to the individual patient and has been effectively used in the USA and in some practices in Britain. Patients are rarely sensitive simply to one group of antigens. It is usually a complex situation in which some react predominantly to chemicals, others to foods, and others to inhaled particles, but treatments for alleviating this conditon do exist and are successful. They do not have to be suppressive treatments but are often healing treatments with the use of these minute antigen doses.

Conclusion

In reviewing the immunology of this condition, as so very little has been proven or published, evidence of the origin has had to be culled from a knowledge of the epidemiology of the subject. Epidemiology is the study of the incidence of the condition as it occurs in populations, and this gives a clue as to whether the condition is restricted, as it is in ME, to outbreaks in particular areas. If this sort of outbreak occurs it is likely to be due to a local infection, either Coxsackie viruses or polio virus epidemics. This has therefore delineated a field which has to be explored and although confirmation of the virus origin has not been clearly obtained, there are indications that viruses are involved. The means of correcting the condition that ensues, which is often a relapsing one, is to control the malfunctioning immunological system which has resulted. Some of the ways of managing the condition have been recorded, though it is not suggested that these are the only ones. It is important to look into nutritional and constitutional factors in a person's make-up. Levels of vitamins and minerals are deficient in some patients who have this complaint and it may be worthwhile pursuing investigation of these. However, there are abnormalities of the functioning of the immune system cells, and means by which these can be restored to normality have been suggested, although tests have not been done in sufficient numbers to establish whether this is something that occurs in all ME sufferers.

Methods of management of a condition can also help to clarify a diagnosis. In a crude form this can be described as follows: if someone has abdominal pain, they are operated upon and have the appendix removed, and their abdominal pain ceases. It is most likely that some inflammatory condition of the appendix has resulted in the abdominal pain; the treatment, which is removal, has effected a cure. In the same way, active treatment can sometimes mitigate symptoms in patients and by inference the cause of the condition can then be assumed. This has been the case in allergy management of some patients who have responded dramatically to treatment. Although this chapter is primarily concerned with the immunological basis of the problem, it has had to impinge on treatment and is giving a view point which has been held concerning the condition, which is one of maladaptation to the environment secondary to a virus-induced illness.

4 DIAGNOSIS AND DIFFERENTIAL DIAGNOSIS

At the moment there is no specific diagnostic test for ME. Diagnosis rests on bearing the illness in mind, careful history-taking and the exclusion of other illnesses.

In the history, the points to look for are a positive family history of allergy; friends or other members of the family affected at the same time, even if their symptoms were not identical; excessive fatigue; muscle twitching; pain in the back of the neck (aching in quality and worse when tired); difficulty in standing and difficulty in lifting heavy weights or raising the arms above the head, that is so-called proximal muscle weakness. Fluctuation of symptoms from day to day and at different times of the day is almost diagnostic, though it does occur also in patients with food allergies. Mood swings and loss of memory and concentration are other important features. It is worth asking the patient if he has difficulty in writing a letter. ME patients frequently have this difficulty and prefer communicating by telephone. Attacks of faintness when hungry or if physical effort has tired the patient out are also characteristic of ME. The unpleasant symptoms may include weakness and giddiness, nausea, sweating, irritability and an intense hunger. These hypoglycaemic attacks due to a low blood sugar can also occur, though less often, in patients with coeliac disease, a disease of malabsorption which will be discussed more fully later.

Marked pallor and puffiness of the eyes on 'off' days or during relapses is almost diagnostic, and relatives can usually tell at once when the patient is unwell by looking at his face. Patients may also have a subnormal rather than a raised temperature and a low blood pressure. Spontaneous bruising may also occur during relapses. If there is a history of an acute attack of sickness and diarrhoea, or sore throat, cough and cold about six weeks before the onset of ME, this is an important diagnostic finding and might help to differentiate the disorder from a heart attack or acute surgical emergency.

Blood tests including the erythrocyte sedimentation rate (ESR) are usually normal in ME, but a muscle enzyme test called the hydroxy butyric dehydrogenase may indicate that there is muscle damage and the illness is not functional. Liver function tests are seldom abnormal except at the onset when clinical signs of jaundice may be absent, but they should be done in spite of absence of fever, particularly if the liver is enlarged or there is prolonged loss of appetite and malaise.

In chronic cases, a history of extreme fatigue with remissions and relapses occurring if work is resumed too soon or following inter-current infection is characteristic. Some cases may be very hard to differentiate from multiple sclerosis, but the severity of muscle pain and the encephalitic features (such as loss of memory and concent-ration) may point to ME. However, lumbar puncture findings may be negative in both illnesses and a normal cerebrospinal fluid tends to support the diagnosis of ME. ME may also be hard to differen-tiate from another disease of muscle weakness called myasthenia gravis, but a special test called the Tensilon test should be positive in the latter illness.

If muscle weakness and fatiguability are more prominent than muscle pain, polymyositis may be suspected and if the ESR is normal, it may be necessary to do a muscle biopsy to differentiate. The illness can also be confused with myxoedema which is due to a lack of the thyroid hormone, but blood tests should differentiate. Likewise, a rare disease of heart muscle, chronic myocarditis, may present with extreme fatigue rather than pains in the chest and an ECG and chest X-ray may be necessary in order to confirm the diagnosis.

A generalised autoimmune disease, systemic lupus erythematosis (SLE), may present with neurological and/or psychiatric symptoms long before the cells characteristic of it are found in the blood stream. But in this disease, the ESR is raised, so this may distinguish it from ME. In addition, patients with SLE have a typical butterfly rash on the face and are sensitive to sunlight. The same symptoms may also be found in a malabsorption syndrome called coeliac disease. Features such as recurrent mouth ulcers, a sore tongue, pallor, abdominal distension, excessive flatulence, abdominal pain and abnormal bowel movements may occur (patients with coeliac disease often have floating stools which are difficult to flush away and which have an unpleasant smell), as well as proximal muscle weakness which may be a complication of the illness. In case of doubt, the patient may be referred to hospital for a special test on the lining (mucous membrane) of the small intestine.

The question of one or more food allergies should also be consi-dered, either as a result of the illness or separately. Features to look for are a family or personal history of allergy, marked fluctuation of symptoms, or the patient himself noticing that he has gone off foods he formerly liked such as milk, eggs, cheese, and so on.

Pain in the back radiating down one or both legs is one of the commonest presentations of the illness and the fluctuation of the symptoms should distinguish it from a prolapsed intervertebral disc. The absence of a history of preceding trauma, but instead the presence of a possible virus infection with diarrhoea and sickness or a sore throat and cold or cough, should alert the doctor to the possibility of ME. Other common presentations of ME are the sudden onset of pain in the chest or stomach. If the former is present and associated with pallor, debility and a low blood pressure, it may be mistaken for a coronary, but the ECG should differentiate. If the ECG is normal,the chest X-ray may show an enlarged heart suggesting a virus infection of the heart muscle, but in many cases both chest X-ray and ECG are normal. However, if the patient still looks and feels ill and has not had previous attacks of angina, the possibility of ME should be considered.

The patient may present as an acute abdominal emergency and surgery may be necessary to exclude appendicitis or some other surgical cause. A viral infection can cause acute appendicitis and should be suspected if there is a predominance of lymphocytes in the blood stream and the total white cell count is not increased. A virus infection can also cause inflammation of the pancreas and many mild cases go undetected, but it should be suspected if the severity of the pain is out of proportion to the physical signs the doctor can elicit on examining the abdomen.

I have seen cases of ME present as a personality disorder in which irritability (characteristically worse before meals, when the patient is hypoglycaemic) and delusions of persecution may be the predominant features. But if there is also loss of appetite, fatigue, loss of memory, insomnia, clumsiness and difficulty in standing, or a preceding history of viral infection, ME should be suspected and other features of the illness such as muscle twitching, pain in the back of the neck and muscle weakness sought.

If one member of a family has had to be referred to a neurologist for vague symptoms such as giddiness, clumsiness or pins and needles to exclude an early case of multiple sclerosis, it is well worthwhile for the family doctor to follow up that family for at least a year. If the neurologist can find no abnormal physical signs, it does not follow that the symptoms must be functional. The possibility of a virus infection which attacks the central nervous system should be borne in mind and if after an interval of six months or even more, another member of the family presents with ME symptoms, this should confirm the organic nature of the original sufferer's seemingly functional symptoms.

Finally, it should be noted that there is probably a large reservoir of undetected virus infection in the community. The cases of ME that we do see are only the tip of the iceberg and it is probable that, as with polio, the vast majority of cases have the illness so slightly that it is mistaken for a severe attack of flu. We only see the patients that do not recover, but if ME is anything like polio, 80 per cent have the illness without paralysis and only a small percentage of the remaining 20 per cent have permanent muscle damage. Indeed, Behan *et al.* (1985) report that, 'our experience is that when general practitioners are aware of the disease it is diagnosed more commonly than motor neurone disease (one per 100,000) and as commonly as multiple sclerosis (three per 100,000).

5 TREATMENT AND MANAGEMENT

Unfortunately at the moment, there is no specific cure for ME, but the following suggestions may help to alleviate some of the symptoms.

Fatigue is a constant feature and the experience of many patients is that standing, which is much more tiring than walking, aggravates this problem. If the patient has to stand, he should try shifting his feet around or whistling or singing under his breath. It is important to avoid standing around in queues and shopping expeditions are better left unfinished than completed if they leave him exhausted. If he forces himself to go on when he is already worn out, he may find that he has to spend not only that evening in bed, but the following ones as well. One medical paper described this classic muscle fatigue in the following way; 'When the patient has walked 100 yards, his muscles feel and behave as though he has just completed a four-minute mile'.

Adequate rest is essential, but it is best for the patient to work out his timetable for himself. If he finds he can watch his favourite television programme late at night by having a rest after lunch, this is fine, but for housewives with family responsibilities it may not be practical. The patient has to learn to walk the difficult path between getting enough exercise and too much, and he is the only person who can decide on what is the right amount for him, bearing in mind the golden rule: when exhausted, stop, even if it does mean leaving the party early. If the arm muscles are exhausted after doing the ironing or too much typing, the patient should try exercising the leg muscles instead, for instance by going for a walk. If he feels dreadful when he first gets up in the morning it may be due to postural hypotension, that is the blood pressure being slow to adjust to the upright position. It may be greatly helped by raising the head of the bed or sleeping on an extra pillow.

Another classic feature that many (but not all) patients complain of is feeling ill if they are hungry, or if muscular effort has tired them out. These unplesant symptoms of tiredness, faintness and irritability are best avoided by taking small meals at regular intervals supplemented by drinks of milk or tea or coffee with plenty of sugar inbetween (every 2 hours if necessary). If this is impractical, and the sufferer wants something to take to work, barley sugars or glucose tablets (which can be bought at any chemist/drug store) are a suitable alternative. Gastric upsets, with loss of appetite, nausea and stomach pains (which can be severe) are a common feature of relapses and 'bad days' with many patients. If the pain does not respond to analgesics, such as paracetamol, a hot water bottle can be tried, preferably combined with a sedative from the doctor. Rich and fried foods, strong seasonings, spices, curries and raw salad vegetables such as cucumber, radishes and spring onions should be avoided at these times. Instead, the patient should be tempted to eat with a light diet of fish, mince and eggs, and yoghurt is a useful standby if he can eat nothing else.

Some patients find that they cannot take alcohol, or that tobacco, coffee, chocolates or cheese upsets them. Others cannot tolerate sunlight. But I would not advise a patient to avoid these things unless he has found that they upset him. It is important not to impose unnecessary restrictions on a life possibly already severely limited by disease. A classic feature of the illness, which is almost diagnostic, is the dramatic variations in the patient's mood and capabilities on 'good' and 'bad' days. The temptation for relatives to think that if he can walk a certain distance one day, the patient must be able to do so on another, is a strong one, but it must be resisted. So must the impulse to think it is all psychological or hysterical and the patient must make more of an effort or try harder.

Symptoms like depression, insomnia and loss of concentration and memory which impair mental powers may be resented, but although these are psychological symptoms, they are caused by an organic virus infection of the brain and spinal cord. So are the mood swings which are such a distressing symptom for many patients, particularly if combined with agitation or undue irritability. Recent research has shown that anti-depressants act by supplying a missing chemical ingredient, tryptophan, which is necessary for the proper functioning of the brain. The patient should not feel that he is 'giving in' if these are prescribed for him, nor need he feel guilty about having to take sleeping tablets. Both the depression and insomnia in this illness are almost certainly due to chemical disturbances in the messengers of the brain, that is the neurotransmitter substances, which we do not yet fully understand. A note of caution here may not come amiss. If the patient has been on tranquillisers for some time, he should not stop them suddenly, as withdrawal symptoms may be acute. Instead, a reduction should be made gradually under the supervision of a doctor. Self-help groups can also give advice and support.

A word now on the perplexing and controversial subject of food allergies. The possibility of one or more allergies must be considered if the patient or his family have a proven history of allergy, particularly if both sides of the family are affected. Allergic illnesses include asthma, hayfever, eczema (particularly in children), allergic rhinitis or nasal polyps, reactions to insect bites or drugs or substances like elastoplast, perfumed soap or particular foods. The symptoms of a food allergy are very like the symptoms of ME and in some cases may be indistinguishable. But if the patient has abdominal distension, excessive flatulence, abnormal bowel movements, stomach pains and a sensation of fullness after eating a small meal, mouth ulcers and a sore tongue the diagnosis of ME is worthy of consideration. Food allergies may also cause central nervous symptoms like fatigue, depression, insomnia, mood swings, loss of memory and concentration, and headaches.

If the patient thinks that certain foods do affect him — the commonest ones are cereals, milk, cheese, eggs, chocolate, red wine and coffee — it is worth leaving out the offending product for a period of 4–6 weeks to see whether he feels any better or is worse when the food is reintroduced into the diet. A clue as to which food it might be that is causing the problem could be that it is something he previously enjoyed, for instance a glass of milk. The trouble with food allergies is that they are frequently multiple and often involve so-called 'masked' allergies, that is foods that one is 'addicted' to and eats very frequently. In this type of allergy the symptoms are delayed and may not come on until 12 hours or so afterwards and are then only relieved when one eats it again. For this type of allergy the only cure is to go on a so-called Stone-Age or exclusion diet in which almost all foods are removed and then gradually reintroduced to see if they cause a reaction. This is a severe test and should only be undertaken with the help of a doctor, but it is encouraging that many ME patients who have tried this treatment report substantial improvement and one patient having been confined to bed was able to resume part-time duties as a nurse.

It should not be forgotten that substances other than foods can also cause allergies and it may be wise to look into the possibility that they may be at fault. Such allergies include drugs (although in this case the patient is usually warned by the appearance of a rash), the house dust mite, hair spray, cosmetics (particularly make-up), perfumes, scented soap or bubble bath; even toothpaste may upset some people. More rarely petrol or gas fumes or nicotine are the culprits.

Nowadays, the good news is that for food allergies in particular, avoidance is not the only therapy. Desensitisation treatment is available and a person can be desensitised to almost all foods and other chemicals by sublingual drops (that is drops taken under the tongue) or by subcutaneous injections.

It is often a good idea for the patient to keep a diary. Otherwise, if the patient sees his doctor on a 'good' day and is asked how he feels, he is apt to reply 'splendid', or the reverse if it is an 'off' day, which may give the doctor no clear idea of how the patient has been feeling in the period since he last saw him since the patient's judgement in discussing his illness is coloured by the previous few days rather than the last few months. I myself keep a graph in which I classify my state of health from A+ to C−. This way, one can have a check as to whether, for example, vitamin B12 injections, evening primrose oil or vitamin C really did help or whether the improvement was just imagined. The patient can also gauge more precisely the effect of increasing or decreasing the dose of, say, anti-depressant if he has a base-line from which to work. It is also useful for him to be able to look back to the previous year and see if an anti-flu vaccination, for instance, upset him then. It is also a great consolation on 'bad' days to look back and see that such periods never lasted for more than ten days, and to see how rapidly the A+ state was regained.

Factors which have been found to trigger off relapses in multiple sclerosis are infection, the puerperium or pregnancy itself, the contraceptive pill, heat, fatigue, alcohol, accidental injury, surgery and anaesthesia, dentistry, diagnostic procedures and emotional upset. It would not be unreasonable to assume that the same factors were operative in ME. Therefore, patients should whenever possible avoid immunisations and female patients should wait at least a year after a relapse before embarking on a pregnancy. There is no known risk that she will transfer the illness to her child, but it is worth having regular check-ups to make sure that there are no central nervous system abnormalities such as spina bifida or hydrocephalus in the fetus, which can nowadays be detected at a very early stage.

Patients with ME are often abnormally sensitive to drugs that act on the central nervous system. But if painful muscle spasms, particularly at night, are a problem, they may well be helped by a small dose of an anti-spasmodic agent like Trancopal, diazepam, Buclofen or Dantrium. But it is advisable to start anti-depressants like Tryptizol on a low dose of say 10 mg tds before gradually working up to the full dose of 25 mg tds. As with multiple sclerosis, numerous treatments have been recommended for ME by some authorities but none has stood the test of controlled clinical trials. Vitamin B12 injections may give relief during a relapse (and are well worth trying even in the absence of anaemia) and evening primrose oil, niacin, pyridoxine, vitamin C, zinc, and so on all have their advocates. If the patient is on a satisfactory diet (low fat, high protein is a good one) and has plenty of fresh vegetables there is no reason to suppose that he may be deficient in any of these nutrients, but they do no harm either and if he thinks that they help, then they probably do, even if it is merely a placebo effect.

6 RESEARCH POSSIBILITIES

I have recently been reading *The Biochemistry of Schizophrenia and Addiction*, edited by Gwynneth Hemmings (MTP Press, Lancaster, 1980). What, you may well ask, has ME to do with schizophrenia, or alcohol addiction for that matter? ME sufferers are not mad! However, the significance of the book here is that it is taken from papers read at a research symposium in which the Schizophrenia Association brought together experts from all over the world to exchange ideas and criticise each other's work. Schizophrenia is seen in this book primarily as a biological illness in which many systems of the body may be upset by genetic fault, and I think that the same holds true for ME. The research is still only at a preliminary, speculative stage, but it may provide pointers for ME with which it appears to have certain affinities.

I would like to see ME patients investigated in a metabolic unit where it would be possible to keep a check on such things as blood pressure, blood sugar, levels of ACTH and cortisone in the blood and amounts excreted in the urine. Nowadays, it is possible to measure neurotransmitters, that is substances which transmit messages in the brain, such as adrenaline, noradrenaline, dopamine, acetylcholine, serotonin and the recently discovered substance gamma-aminobutyric acid (GABA). This might provide insights into why ME patients can change so dramatically from day to day and at different times of the day. These changes in both mental and physical state are almost diagnostic of ME, though they can also occur in patients with food allergies.

The sort of questions that might be answered would include the following. Why are so many sufferers worse first thing in the morning? Is it due, for example, to a low blood pressure and a slowness to adjust to the upright posture or could a low blood sugar or low cortisol level be at fault? Why are women patients (in common with another central nervous system disorder, myasthenia gravis) worse premenstrually? Could it be due to fluid retention or a changed relationship between the sex hormones of the body, that is a relative progesterone deficiency? If patients say they have a particular 'low' period, between say 4 and 6 p.m., could it be a mood change induced by a lack of the hormone cortisone or the essential amino acid tryptophan in the blood stream? Diurnal variations occur in the cortisol levels in the blood stream so it is important that cortisone or an immune suppressant is administered at the right time of day.

One of the most interesting symptoms produced by ME patients has so far not been adequately investigated. This is the tendency to develop a low blood sugar (hypoglycaemia) if meals are delayed or if exercise has tired the patient. During the Royal Free Hospital outbreak, one patient was admitted in a hypoglycaemic coma and another doctor-patient said that if she took a sherry before a meal she was rendered more or less unconscious. Random blood sugars taken from ME patients at times when they complain of hypoglycaemic symptoms such as faintness, nausea, irritability and an intense hunger have proved inconclusive. But patients frequently have abnormal glucose tolerance tests, and we need to study individual patterns of behaviour and see how much the blood sugar varies from what is normal for that patient.

The role of the pancreas in this illness could be crucial. Many patients present with severe stomach pain thought to be psychosomatic because of the apparent absence of confirmatory physical signs. But this is typical of acute pancreatitis. Professor William Philpott of Oklahoma has suggested that the pancreas may be a primary target organ in cases of autoimmune disease. If a virus (like that causing mumps for example) attacks the pancreas, there may be a deficiency of pancreatic juices so that proteins are inadequately digested. They may therefore pass through the lining of the small intestine as undigested particles, and as such be attacked by the white cells in the patient's blood stream as foreign bodies. The resulting large particle is called an immune-complex and may cause blockage of the small blood vessels in the brain and elsewhere. This would explain the protean symptomatology of ME (which has led so many doctors to dismiss sufferers as hypochondriacs), and make symptoms such as noises in the ears or a bad taste in the mouth respectable, since the symptom produced would be dependant on the site at which the blood vessel was blocked.

Professor Philpott's theory would also explain how a virus infection can trigger off a food allergy. For instance, a patient could develop a headache after eating cheese because the protein was not being broken down by pancreatic juices to its constituent amino acids. A blood sugar taken at the same time, if raised, would support the theory of insufficient insulin from the pancreas. Some

ME patients develop a craving for sugar at certain times, and this could be due to a fluctuation in insulin levels.

Many ME patients report symptoms such as abdominal distension, discomfort after food, excessive flatulence and irregular bowel movements typical of a malabsorption syndrome. In coeliac disease, a malabsorption illness caused by an intolerance to the wheat protein gluten, patients also complain of typical ME symptoms such as pallor, puffiness of the eyes, coldness of the extremities, hypoglycaemic attacks, undue tiredness, muscle weakness (giving rise to difficulty in standing or raising the arms above the head) and psychological symptoms. Chronic pancreatitis may present either with diabetes mellitus or as a malabsorption syndrome, and since ME patients frequently have symptoms common to both, this provides further evidence that the pancreas may be implicated.

In the book referred to at the beginning of this chapter the section on immunological reactions of psychotic patients to fractions of gluten, states that not only does gluten react with and damage the intestinal lining in coeliac patients, but also in certain susceptible individuals gluten may interfere with normal biological processes in the brain as well, causing psychotic symptoms. Coeliac disease occurs in schizophrenia and vice versa far more often than might be expected on the basis of chance. A recent report stated that 54 per cent of a group of mentally ill patients had antibodies to cereal proteins compared with 19 per cent of the control group. These observations led Dohan to conclude that schizophrenia and hypersensitivity to gluten share one or more common genes, and that the differences in the two diseases could be determined by the dissimilar components of the respective gene complexes.

In another chapter of the same book, Professor D. F. Horrobin and others suggest that the fundamental problem in schizophrenia may be a low ratio of the prostaglandins (chemicals produced by the body which are, among other functions, concerned with the production of inflammation and changes in the size of blood vessels) to the activity of the neurotransmitter substance dopamine. Horrobin suggests elimination of possible dietary deficiencies (which could cause less dopamine or prostaglandins to be produced) by taking higher than the minimal recommended daily doses of certain substances. Thus, he says that taking 4–6 ml of evening primrose oil, pyridoxine 100–200 mg, zinc 20–40 mg, vitamin C 1–2 g and niacin (a B vitamin) 100–200 mg per day should be adequate to ensure that no deficiencies are present. Would the same approach be worth trying in ME?

It would be interesting if more evidence was available — to see how susceptible ME patients were to other illnesses, in case this threw more light on the nature of the disease. Thus there seems to be an increased incidence of arthritis in ME whereas in schizophrenia it is fairly well established that the incidence is reduced. The same applies to gynaecological disorders which appear to be increased in ME patients but reduced in schizophrenia. However, it is worth noting that if they do occur in schizophrenics, the hormone imbalance causes the amount of depression to be significantly increased.

So far not many ME patients have been tissue-typed. But if we had more material to work on it would be interesting to see whether ME patients possessed the same HLA antigens (that is, the antigens found to be important in transplantation surgery) as multiple sclerosis patients. These antigens are important because they are associated with genes which determine the character, intensity and duration of immune responses. Patients with ankylosing spondylitis (a rare inflammatory disease of the spine) have already been found to possess the same antigens as multiple sclerosis patients.

ME also has similarities with porphyria, the hereditary disease suffered by the Hanoverian monarchs. The combination of physical symptoms such as muscle weakness and abdominal pain with mental symptoms like hallucinations would suggest a metabolic disorder. A doctor-patient has reported an aggravation of her abdominal pain when barbiturates were prescribed in hospital after an operation. The same patient has reported on the presence of large fatty stools (steatorrhea) during a relapse when all she could eat was yoghurt, suggesting a disorder of fat metabolism. The role of zinc is also worthy of consideration in any research into the metabolism of this illness.

J.M. Littleton in a chapter on alchoholism and schizophrenia in *The Biochemistry of Schizophrenia and Addiction*, discusses the fat or lipid metabolism of the cell membrane. He says that the ability of organisms to alter fats in nerve cell membranes fits the bill as a fundamental process which may be influenced by genes, diet, age and hormones, and which could produce changes in a variety of neurotransmitter-related substances and enzymes. Another suggestion is that substances on the surfaces of nerve cells (i.e. antigens), could be altered by persistent virus infection so that some, which are normally repressed, are expressed outside the cell. These altered antigens could induce the proliferation of the so-called T lymphocytes, and these T lymphocytes can readily be detected in excess in another autoimmune disorder, systemic lupus erythematosis. This disease has an undisputed autoimmune origin and can present with psychological symptoms. I once heard a specialist in immunology say that he had cured a patient with this disease not by the prescription of cortisone (the standard treatment) but by removing her from her job, which was that of a hairdresser. Thus either allergy or an infection can trigger off autoimmune reactions. Feldberg, in 1976, postulated that schizophrenia may be associated with increased production of prostaglandin in certain parts of the brain. But ME appears more likely to be due to an imbalance between the various neurotransmitter substances in the brain. It is of interest that one ME patient was admitted to hospital because it was thought that he was suffering from a carcinoid (i.e. a neurotransmitter producing tumour), but at operation nothing was found.

All the evidence we possess at present suggests that many different viruses may precipitate the illness. In particular the Epstein and Barr (EB) or glandular fever virus is frequently implicated and this can itself cause neurological symptoms in a severe attack. Other viruses found to trigger off the illness are Coxsackie B, echo 17, hepatitis and polio viruses and, more rarely, chicken pox and mumps. It is interesting that the onset of insulin-dependant diabetes (particularly in children) has been linked with a viral attack, and that the disease often presents in September, October or January to February when viral infection is at its most prevalent. It is now widely accepted that diabetes is another autoimmune disease triggered off by a virus.

Some of the latest research findings on ME were presented at a symposium held in Cambridge in September 1983. The ME Association's newsletter carries this report from Dr Peter Behan, Consultant Neurologist and Reader in Neurology at the Institute of Neurological Sciences, Glasgow, which I have summarised as follows:

> Dr Jamal from our department using a highly specialised technique, nuclear magnetic resonance, demonstrated that the majority of patients had abnormalities of their muscle . . . Patients with the disease have an abnormality of using oxygen in

their muscles. This seems to be connected with a disorganisation of utilisation of oxygen and sugar.

We have not only measured the neutralising antibody but looked at a specific antibody, i.e. immunoglobulin M, which if present and specific strongly suggests that the patient has recently come in contact with the virus, or more importantly, carries the virus and is chronically infected.

We furthermore were able to demonstrate that there was impaired regulation of the immune system in patients with the disease both in the acute and chronic stage. The abnormality was that of a mild to moderate type of immune deficiency; the sort that is found in persistent virus infection . . . It is therefore particularly exciting to know that we now have, albeit on the research side, a method of demonstrating abnormalities in patients in whom years ago without such advanced techniques, a diagnosis of hysteria would almost certainly have been made. It is important to understand that the techniques used are sophisticated, advanced, and only available on a research basis. They do open up the possibility of understanding the illness in greater depth and of allowing us to think now about ways of approaching therapy.

In a recent scientific paper, Behan and his colleagues (1985) report the results of examining 50 patients, as follows:

The results reported here suggest that the syndrome is due to the interaction of viral infection and immunological processes which produce damage to intracellular enzymes and result in abnormal muscle metabolism, especially on exercise. Viral infections have already been shown to cause such enzyme abnormalities. Another possibility is that an autoantibody such as the anti-mitochondrial antibody recently identified in patients with viral myocarditis, might be involved. We conclude that further study of the postviral fatigue syndrome and elucidation of the pathogenic mechanisms involved will have important implications not only for patients with this syndrome but also for those with other postviral neurological illnesses.

One might add that if we can unlock the key of ME, we might also unravel the mystery of multiple sclerosis, schizophrenia, coeliac disease, myasthenia gravis and diabetes.

PART TWO:

TYPICAL CASE HISTORIES

CASE HISTORY 1: ANATOMY OF AN ILLNESS

A Doctor-Patient (M.W.)

Depressive illness seems to be a fashionable diagnosis these days. More and more it is being used as an umbrella term to explain everything from psychotic behaviour to somatic symptoms for which there appears to be no other obvious explanation. Readers must judge for themselves whether they think it is the right label for the illness described below which could more accurately be defined as a severe relapse of ME had the hospital concerned believed that such an entity existed!

I entered hospital just before Christmas feeling something of a fraud. I thought I was only mildly depressed and my chief symptom was colicky abdominal pain, aggravated by food, in addition to my pre-existing muscle fatiguability and weakness of the legs. Christmas in hospital is supposed to be fun, but for me it was a time of minor frustrations. The library was closed and so was the bank, so no change was obtainable for the telephone. Then first the 2p and then the 10p slots on the trolley jammed, and could not be unblocked until after the holiday. But for me it was also a time of heightened awareness; my chrysanthemums had never appeared more beautiful, and a piece of Mozart fleetingly heard on a transistor radio was unbearably poignant. Some nurses' compassion was moving to behold, but some patients' cases were so tragic it made me rage against so cruel a Creator.

When over the holiday period no one bothered to take my TPR or blood pressure or enquire about my bowels, I thought it was because my case was hopeless, and they were no longer interested. When this was followed by the suggestion that I could go home the next day, I imagined it was because the condition, whether due to adhesions or a tumour, was inoperable and I was to be sent home to die.

How annoying it was for a doctor-patient to be told that all the blood tests were satisfactory without being given details. Perhaps this was why I strained my ears to hear what was being said about me through half-closed doors. Suddenly the illness became psychotic. I thought other patients and staff were constantly talking about me, and words like 'inoperable', 'neurotic', 'tumour', 'carcinoid', 'poor thing', 'does she know?', 'of course she knows', echoed through the half-closed door. The only way I could drown these 'voices' was by putting on the radio or TV because with the door closed they were even worse. When I felt well enough, I could escape by talking to the patients in the next ward, but on a 'bad' day my legs were too weak to walk that far. Fears, however irrational, were worse at night; in the morning I thought my intestinal obstruction was due to adhesions (which I had had before), but at night it was carcinoma of the colon. In reality, I think I had developed a medical paralytic ileus, for I lost my appetite completely and the abdominal pain became much more severe.

In desperation one evening, I took 10 mgs of Valium because the pain had awakened me, and the nurses were adamant that it was not yet time for repeat Valium or Distalgesic. I recommend all doctors who have the misfortune to become hospital patients to secrete a supply of Valium tablets in their pocket or handbag. The more eminent and renowned the hospital, the more necessary this is, because the rules will be rigidly enforced.

My condition deteriorated alarmingly and I could eat hardly anything; small morsels of bread, two grapes, two teaspoonfuls of raspberry yoghurt and half a cup of tea, are items in the notes I was asked to make about what I had eaten. Any food caused immediate abdominal discomfort and I got the pain at times even when I was not eating. I was convinced that I was dying and needed an intravenous drip immediately. I pleaded with the staff to transfer me to a hospice where at least I thought the pain would be adequately controlled. When my consultant suggested that I ought to have a barium meal and follow-through and then a barium enema, I thought he was mad to suggest such investigations in an obstructed patient. From there it was a short step to my considering that it was Dr X who was mad, not I. I imagined that he had some kind of telepathic communication with me and knew the words that I was about to write in advance of my writing them. I paid him the considerable compliment of thinking that he was a better journalist than me! I even thought my bedside table was bugged, and made a mark on it so that I should know which one it was in the future.

Removal to a four-bedded ward banished most of the voices, though I was hypersensitive to noise and other people's visitors were hell. But there was less privacy in a four-bed unit than in a larger general ward and conversations were easily overheard.

Surprisingly, when I was more ill, I preferred the general ward to the side one because there was more going on to keep me amused. I could not concentrate on reading or writing or even listening to the radio, but my interior dialogue with the 'voices' kept me occupied, and at times I begrudged even going to the toilet for fear of missing something of importance. Not surprisingly, before very long a psychiatrist was called in, and I was transferred to a psychiatric ward. I thought the specialist had come to see not me but Dr X (whom I was convinced had a brain tumour) and wanted my views on how he had behaved to me. I was surprised when Dr X came to see me in the psychiatric ward still in his white coat, because I thought by now he would have been dismissed or sent away for treatment.

Life in the psychiatric ward was at first sheer hell. The nurses seemed to refuse to believe that patients could have physical as well as psychological symptoms. Thus, when I developed acute retention over a weekend, it was not until 7.30 p.m. that I was allowed to see a doctor. A severe attack of colicky lower abdominal pain radiating down both legs woke me at 11.30 one night despite the large dose of Largactil I had been given for night sedation. I was eventually given an injection of Valium, but it recurred with renewed force at 2.30 a.m. One callous nurse actually said that it was an idea I had formed in my mind that I had this pain, and another nurse not only threatened to but actually did remove the buzzer when I kept ringing it. Equally, my complaints of facial pain were ignored and it was only after considerable pressure that I was allowed to see a dentist who confirmed that the pain could be dental in origin, though looking back I think it more likely to have been some kind of trigeminal neuralgia.

The staff refused to believe that at first my legs were too weak to walk as far as the canteen, and when I asked for my stick which inadvertently had been left in the medical ward, I was told that I did not need it. It may have been a junior nurse who said to me, 'You can walk as well as I can, your legs are as good as mine', but the charge nurse was equally adamant that the stick was merely a psychological crutch. It was a great disadvantage for the nurses to wear no uniform because you did not know who you were dealing with, and when I asked for a wheelchair or a commode and it was not forthcoming I had no means of telling whether they refused to give it or simply had not got one.

The ward round was an unnerving experience and I went to it

feeling angry, and hypoglycaemic and determined not to reveal any of my innermost thoughts to the sea of faces confronting me. This was no easy task as I was conscious of my emotional lability: I had already revealed far too much to the medical student assigned to me, and had the greatest difficulty in not blowing kisses to visitors who were mere acquaintances. I also had to resist the temptation to join in other people's conversations with their visitors. When you are acutely ill, you are not aware that you are constantly repeating yourself until you notice it in other patients.

A symptom which was most distressing was an inability to initiate micturition. I was never conscious that I wanted to go to the toilet, only the vague feeling that I ought to try, and then it took so long to get started that I almost abandoned the attempt. This was presumably a Parkinsonian side-effect from the large doses of Largactil I was receiving, as were grimacing movements about the mouth, a tremor of the lower lip, dilated pupils and flecks of saliva at the corners of the mouth, particularly if I had been doing a lot of talking. Harder to explain were several attacks of palpitations which were rather alarming, a splitting headache one morning, muscle twitching in my shoulder muscles at times and oedema under the eyes. I was always very hungry for breakfast, and felt much better after food which seemed to revive me.

The first letter I wrote after five and a half weeks in hospital was a minor triumph. I could not see clearly enough to fill in a cheque nor could I explain the nature of my toothache when I saw the dentist. I found I was searching for the right word and articulation was difficult. I could not say the word cytomegalovirus on one occasion, and on others I would come out with the word 'bra' instead of 'cardigan' which added to my difficulties in communication.

In all I spent about three months in hospital, and took at least as long to get over the illness. It was a long time before I was strong enough to join in the physical activities that were the staple diet of life in a psychiatric unit. It is arguable whether if rest had been the basis of my treatment, instead of forced exertion at an early stage, the illness would have terminated more quickly or run a more benign course.

CASE HISTORY 2

A Nightmare Experience (B.W.)

The illness began insidiously. If I sat out in the garden reading a book and heard the sound of children's laughter, I was convinced that they were laughing at me. As a medical journalist, writing was important to me, and I was concerned that my articles should be read only by my friends. Normally, I thought they were safe from the prying eyes of my mother in a locked suitcase, but now the keys had to be lodged with a friend down the road for added safety.

At first I did not recognise these as mental symptoms, but when I was confined to bed with a flu-like illness, I realised something must be wrong. Now mental and physical symptoms combined to assail me and I lost my appetite completely. On one occasion when my GP called to see me, she stuck a thermometer in my mouth at the same time asking me to take deep breaths, so that she could examine my chest. I found this hilarious, all the more so since she could not see the joke, but when I tried to tell the hospital staff that I thought it was the funniest thing since 'Fawlty Towers', they merely thought me hysterical.

I imagined my mother had taken the telephone off the hook because she was fed up with people enquiring after my health. I rang up my cousin to tell him this and to warn him not to worry if he could not get through. He sounded embarrassed, and I imagine it was because he had to take this bizarre message in the full hearing of his receptionist. I believed that my mother not only listened in to my telephone calls on an upstairs extension, but also read through my letters. Thus when an eagerly awaited letter from an American professor was delayed I imagined my mother had held it back until a particularly bad day when she wished to cheer me up.

I was almost sure my doctor had realised how ill I was and that hospital admission was necessary, but that my mother had sent the ambulance away, saying she was able to look after her daughter at home. She said this because she was in her 80s, and frightened of being left alone in the house. I remember shouting 'Send for Dr T.' at the top of my voice, hoping that the neighbours would hear, and knowing that Dr T. was a respected GP who worked in our area.

Eventually, I crawled from bed, dialled 999 on the upstairs phone and implored the man who answered to send for an ambulance to take me to Banstead Lodge, where I had been treated previously, so they would have ready access to my notes. I doubted whether he would oblige, particularly since Banstead Lodge was not the nearest hospital, but when I said the diagnosis was viral encephalitis, he sounded concerned. I must have looked as ill as I felt because when the ambulance men did arrive, they asked no questions, but rushed me straight to hospital.

I was kept waiting for what seemed like an eternity in the casualty department, presumably while they were trying to decide what to do with me. I was asked if I wanted a cup of tea, but when it came it always contained milk, so I could not drink it. At that time I believed that I had multiple food allergies to gluten, cereals, milk, eggs, cheese and beef, so that at home I lived on hardly anything except fish, fruit and lamb. Although this experimental diet had originally been prescribed by the hospital, the nurses simply thought I was quite mad and that my food fads were impossible to satisfy. I was eventually taken to a ward which I did not realise was a psychiatric one. I was seized by severe stomach pains for which the only remedy was to lie completely still. After what seemed like a long interval, a doctor came to examine me, and ordered an immediate X-ray; the strange fact about the pain was that it improved as soon as I sat upright in the X-ray chair, so I thought the nurses must have imagined that I was pretending again.

My illness was such a traumatic experience that even now I find it hard to give a lucid account of it. Nights were terrible. I was given nothing to help me sleep, but one Stelazine tablet which had no discernible effect. I spent some nights constantly ringing the bell and calling for sleeping tablets or tea which seldom came. Sometimes I was made to get up and sit in the corridor, and on one occasion I asked if I could join in a game of scrabble, but then found I was too ill to concentrate. On another occasion I was given a drink which I was convinced contained milk to test whether I was truly allergic to it. I had to be forced to drink the stuff, and likewise struggled against what was probably a tranquilising injection, but which at the time I firmly believed was gluten, again given to test the reaction.

I imagined I was in a neurosurgical ward, being subtly assessed as to whether I had an operable brain tumour. The assessment included doctors monitoring my behaviour night and day through a peephole in the wall behind my bed. I imagined they sat there with a panel of instruments before them, and could follow my movements even into the toilet. I thought at least two of the other patients were nurses in disguise, who had been sent from Queen's Square (through the good offices of a friend I knew working there) to observe my behaviour and prevent any ill treatment. I even imagined another patient, who was in reality a secretary, was a correspondent from *The Guardian* writing up my story for her paper. I also believed the BBC was in on the act, which I imagined had attracted worldwide interest.

I had no sense of time, and thought the clocks had been tampered with specifically to confuse me. I thought that a television programme had been selected especially for me, because it dealt with jobs available for people who had become disabled, for example in the pathology laboratory. On the other hand, even when I was feeling better watching a TV horror serial terrified me, and even the colours on a TV set were at first too bright for my unaccustomed eyes. The noise of the vacuum cleaner literally went through me, and at first I thought it was being done deliberately to see how much noise I could stand. When I saw two orderlies put glasses into the pockets of their overalls, I thought they were stealing them, and mentally resolved to take even more care of my belongings (I had already decided to sleep with my briefcase under my pillow if I went for an operation). As it was, valuables such as purse, pen, chequebook, keys and scissors had mysteriously been removed from my handbag, and I was uncertain as to whether my mother or the hospital authorities were responsible. It was irritating not even to have a pair of scissors to cut my nails, though I soon discovered I was far too shaky to manage this alone and was only too glad of the help of one of the few nurses kind enough to assist me.

I was convinced that I needed an urgent operation for a brain tumour and was scared of eating anything, even as few as six grapes, in case the operation had to be postponed. I kept seeing what appeared to be a surgical trolley come and go at the end of my ward. I was convinced one of the house officers looking after me was in fact a medical student and did not know his job. I refused to talk to a psychologist at the end of the day, because I wanted to husband my resources for the more important visitors I imagined were queueing up to see me. I thought half the world was enquiring after me, but they were not allowed in and their messages were being prevented from reaching me.

In fact, sometimes I was too ill to see any visitors, and when a close friend arrived one night I was forced to send her away, because the only way I could remain comfortable was by not moving. I refused to see my mother because I thought she was senile, and I can remember saying that I would only see her if she went on a gluten-free diet (which I had read was sometimes successful in presenile dementia) and was admitted as a voluntary patient to a mental hospital. She was not the only person I thought in need of a gluten-free diet. I considered my consultant was also a coeliac patient, which would explain his 'peculiar behaviour'. Various other doctors or consultants I came across were all to my mind equally mad, or too emotionally involved with me to give me an injection, set up a drip, or decide on a positive course of action.

I was convinced that all the nursing staff were ranged against me. One morning, for instance, I had the most severe stomach pain, but nobody did anything about it. It felt as though it was due to acute retention of urine, and I begged the nurses to pass a catheter or get a doctor. I felt the pain was so severe that it would only respond to morphia, but when she did belatedly arrive, the doctor refused to give me anything. I imagined absurdly that grimacing movements of my mouth, which I was unable to control were preventing the doctors from giving me any medication, and that if only I could control my expression, and perhaps manage a smile, I would get the longed for relief. In the afternoon, in spite of my still not being able to go to the toilet, I was surprisingly able to forget totally the pain in the only enjoyable time of my stay. I have no idea whether I was sitting on the bed or walking about, talking out loud or merely to myself, but I seemed to be engaged in a rapturous telepathic conversation with my vicar, my former psychiatrist, a neurologist, and a well known liver specialist from another hospital, who had briefly seen me. My vicar told me he was going to divorce his wife and marry me, and the psychiatrist said she too was a writer, and wrote under the pseudonym of a Sunday journalist who I had long admired. My 'voices' were agreed that the message I was charged to take back with me was that it was only love that made the world go round.

The pain had gone when I returned from my reverie, but I saw a male nurse use the patients' toilet which irritated me because I thought he did it on purpose, knowing that I could not follow suit. Eventually, later in the evening, I was able to pass a little urine which appeared blood stained, indicating that I was either having visual as well as auditory hallucinations, or that I had passed a small kidney stone.

Most of the time I lay on my back trying to stop 'the shakes'. It seemed as if I was engaged in a life and death struggle, and the only way to win it was to keep still. There were times, gazing out through the small window in my cell-like room, when I thought I would never leave the hospital. I had to force myself to keep still to stop the constant shaking, yet if I allowed myself to fall asleep, I thought I would never wake. This could have been the result of coming off the drugs to which I had become accustomed, but it seemed to be similar to 'the bends', deep sea divers experience when they return too quickly to the surface, or like the delerium tremens of alcoholics when they are being 'dried out'. I imagined cold air was being pumped into my room to lower the oxygen requirements of my 'overheated' brain. But when the window was left open on one occasion and I was too weak to close it, I nearly froze with cold. I could not understand why the nurses did not realise that I was in a condition of status epilepticus, and did not give me an injection to stop it. A Stelazine tablet by mouth only seemed to make the shaking worse. They paid no attention either to my bowels, which gave me a constant feeling of pressure in the rectum because I was so constipated.

When I was eventually convinced I was not going to have an operation at this hospital, I imagined it was because they did not have adequate neurosurgical facilities, and I begged to be transferred to St Anne's which was newer and I thought better equipped. I hoped to be accompanied by my favourite nurse, who was in fact a patient to whom I had taken a great fancy. She frequently wandered into my room, rearranged the pillows, sang songs or read to me; I was sure she had been given strict instructions not to let me tire myself out by too much talking. Twice I tried to discharge myself, managing with difficulty to form the letters for a short note, but no notice was taken. The shock when I did finally discover that I was in a psychiatric ward with real patients was a major one. Up until then, I had thought the other people there were merely guinea pigs, being asked to test various diets in order to see whether they gave rise to mental symptoms.

Convalescence was a slow process, and at times I was pushed along too fast. On some occasions I was made to sit up in a chair for too long, so that I pleaded to be allowed to go back to bed, and when this was refused had to lie down on the floor in the common room, using a chair cushion as a pillow. Slowly I did recover, and high spots in that recovery were the tastes of simple foods like fish and chips with tomato sauce. I can particularly remember savouring the taste of mayonnaise with salad, because it was a luxury that had been excluded by my diet. In the early days I was always ravenously hungry, and the waiting for the trolleys to appear seemed never ending. Grapes did little to appease my hunger and I could not wait for the others to be served before beginning my meal. Gradually, my numbed senses returned to life. I was allowed home at weekends, but at first I was afraid of my darkened bedroom, and the blankets to which I was unaccustomed seemed too heavy. I had to force myself to leave the now friendly cocoon in which I had spent three months of my life. If it had not been for the fact that my hair needed a perm, it might have been much longer before I could have summoned up the courage to leave the shelter of the hospital and return to normal life.

Is there anything to be learnt from this story? I have told it only in the hope that it might increase the understanding of mental illness among the staff who have to deal with it, and lessen the isolation felt by the patients who live in a nightmare world of delusions and hallucinations.

Editor's Note

These first two harrowing case histories show how great is the suffering when physical and mental symptoms are combined and frequently insufficient attention is paid to the former. A doctor-reader wrote to the editor after the first story appeared in a medical publication noting the close similarity to his experiences as a sufferer of porphyria, but in his case his physical symptoms were taken seriously.

Much of the symptomatology of the patient in case history 2 experienced in hospital could well have been due to the sudden withdrawal of the medication she was taking. Addiction to benzodiazepine drugs has only recently come to be recognised as a medical problem and this history illustrates the profound chemical upset that can be caused in the body by sudden withdrawal.

CASE HISTORY 3

Doctor M.W., Aged 51

I first became ill about 20 years ago. The onset was insidious and the presenting symptom was palpitations. My first instinct was that it was imagination, or the bra was too tight, or it was the cold in the open air theatre in Regent's Park. I was playing a lot of tennis at the time and had a tournament coming up, so I thought it might be as well to see someone before entering, particularly when my partner suggested it might be thyrotoxicosis. The day I was due for the hospital appointment I felt weak and had a vague pain in my left arm. I decided that I was definitely neurotic and that it was absurd to imagine rheumatic fever or angina at my age, I was then 31. This opinion was endorsed by the consultant (though not in so many words) who after a blood test and an ECG, both of which were normal, suggested that perhaps I had been overdoing things and should take a few days rest. I ignored the doctor's advice for fear of alarming my family unnecessarily, and the symptoms duly disappeared of their own accord. This consultation was to have a considerable effect on my future course of action, for though Dr X had been very kind, I felt a bit of a fool. When I did not feel well in the following summer and had only vague symptoms of tiredness to complain of, I felt chary of approaching him again for fear of being labelled neurotic. As I knew him socially and had had him out on several domiciliary visits, it was also a matter of professional pride that he should retain his faith in my clinical judgement. My reaction in the face of increasing lassitude was to go out and play more tennis in order to convince myself that it was purely psychological. It was obvious, even to me by this time that this was not so, as I certainly did not have the energy to play my usual number of tennis sets and tired easily on walks in the country. I remember driving back from a weekend out of town feeling exhausted and being extremely irritable with a friend who expected to be dropped at her home, which I usually did without demur. On reflection I think this was due to hypoglycaemia, though I was not aware of similar symptoms directly attributable to this cause until much later.

In the midst of this chronic illness I developed acute appendicitis.

My recovery after operation was slow, and I was intensely irritated by people who kept telling me they were back to work within three weeks of the operation. I could not understand it myself, as I knew there had been no peritonitis or post-operative complications. I can recall feeling very weak and being unable to stand for any length of time. I also remember one or two attacks of uncontrollable shivering, like a rigor, which rather surprised me.

During the following summer, I felt far from well, but there was nothing definite I could put my finger on. The main symptom was lassitude and fatiguability, but I also had more definite symptoms such as loss of appetite and a distaste for fried foods. I gave up fried egg and bacon for breakfast and could not face fried fish and chips, which had been a useful standby after an exhausting Friday evening surgery. A recurrent conjunctivitis, which various samples from the surgery failed to clear was a mild irritant. A swab grew no organisms, but my eyes continued to smart, particularly when I sat near a fire, or out in the sun, and I changed one item of make-up after another without success, in a vain attempt to find the hidden allergen.

Outings to theatres and concerts were not always the pleasure they used to be, though I think it was not until later that I found myself sitting through plays and concerts feeling so tired that I could not wait for them to end. On one occasion at the Albert Hall I was seized by colicky abdominal pain , which, although not severe when compared with later attacks, was bad enough to interfere with my enjoyment of the second half of the concert. It was accompanied by a feeling of faintness, and when we met with some friends in the corridor in the interval I found I had to lean against the wall for support and longed for the conversation to end. We had had rather an exotic meal at an Italian restaurant beforehand, but I thought surely these were not the symptoms of a peptic ulcer and considered having a barium meal if they continued. There was another occasion when I met a friend for a pre-theatre dinner and felt distinctly odd afterwards. I think it was again faintness and abdominal discomfort and I remember choosing a seat next to the gangway in case I had to go out. It was also about this time that I first detected an intolerance to alcohol and could not understand why I drove home half drunk after a wedding, in which I had had no more than my usual sherry and the toast in champagne. Sometimes these attacks of faintness, nausea and giddiness accompanied by discomfort followed a meal, but they were frequently relieved by passing flatus.

The next episode was at Saltzburg, where I had gone for the festival. We were staying at the picturesque resort of St Gilgen in the Austrian lake district. On emerging from my first swim in the lake, I found I was inexplicably short of breath. This surprised me as I had not been in very long and had not been particularly energetic. I put it down to a lack of training and thought no more about it. Sunbathing a few days later I noticed a rather ugly bruise on my thigh, which I was sure I had not knocked. I could feel palpable glands in both groins and by this time would have been thoroughly alarmed were it not for the fact that a full programme of sightseeing by day and festival visits by night left me little time for worry.

It was not until the second week of the holiday that my abdominal pain recurred and I was forced to miss out on several concerts I had booked for. The pain was aggravated by food and I remember being determined to attend the performance of Così fan tutte, and thinking the only way to do so was to eat nothing beforehand. I did this and enjoyed the first half, but in the second the abdominal pain and faintness returned, and a fellow doctor in the party gave me a glass of brandy and said I looked as white as a sheet. I managed to get back to the hotel, but then had to take to my bed because of the pain, which was accompanied by weakness, loss of appetite and nausea. Friends remarked on my colour, and I thought of infective hepatitis, but it seemed to me more of a pallor than a true jaundice. The symptoms were similar to the appendix episode, and I was glad it was already out otherwise somebody might have suggested having a look.

I could eat hardly any of the Austrian food the hotel sent up and staggered to an adjacent restaurant for scrambled egg. I felt very weak and thought I would never make it, an effect I learnt later to identify with hypoglycaemia. When I got out of bed and started walking, the lake seemed miles away and I had no energy for the souvenir hunting I had intended. A drink by the water's edge seemed to have lost its attraction and, worse still, the lakes surrounded by mountains no longer seemed beautiful. I recovered in time to fly back to England with the rest of the party, but the illness cast its blight over the holiday and it deterred me from taking holidays abroad for a long time. The next major episode was not until three months later. I was doing an afternoon surgery when I had a recurrence of the abdominal pain, more severe than before. It was not eased by any analgesic and was accompanied by diarrhoea of up to six to eight times an hour involving a dash from the telephone on one occasion. I suspected something serious was afoot, and I rang up our secretary who was both a friend and an SRN and she — bless her — said 'come round at once with a nightdress and sponge bag', which I only too gladly did.

I was pretty ill over the weekend and could not eat anything, but attempted a Monday morning surgery. The medical bag felt strangely heavy and I could not cope with the surgery. I went into the drawing room next door and phoned our locum, who fortunately was available straightaway. I somehow realised that this was going to be a long business. I returned to bed, a domiciliary visit was arranged and by the Wednesday I was in a London teaching hospital with a provisional diagnosis of Addison's Disease. The blood pressure was found to be low and the history of abdominal pain and weakness fitted in with this diagnosis. I was only too glad that something treatable had been found and could not wait to start taking the tablets. I was impatient of the delay caused by taking 24-hour specimens and so on, and was surprised that even the test dose of ACTH did not make me feel any better. By that time I was feeling really dreadful and can remember one evening when I literally did not care whether I lived or died. When I was told it was not Addison's disease and that steroids would not help, I felt that I could not live through another week like the last one. It did not need my brother's tentative suggestion that perhaps he should bring my parents back from their overseas holiday, or junior nurses peeping through the door, and then getting someone more senior to see if I was alright to make me realise how ill I was. I already felt as though I were at death's door and all I cared about was that this suffering should cease.

The symptoms were varied and affected most systems of the body. Gastrointestinal ones included profound anorexia and nausea with occasional vomiting. My distaste for foods, particularly fats, was extreme at times and I could not face buttered bread. The most distressing symptom was colicky abdominal pain, severe at times, accompanied by constipation. The latter, aggravated as it was by muscle weakness and unrelieved by enemas, was very trying. Micturition symptoms were oliguria, difficulty in starting and frank retention at times. For the first time, I could sympathise with the elderly patient who keeps asking for a bedpan and then having got it, cannot use it. I realise that this must be very aggravating for the nurses, but is not the patient's fault. I tried running taps and drinking glasses of water while waiting, but found the best solution was to read a magazine, and then if one could become sufficiently immersed to forget the object of the exercise all would eventually be well.

Central nervous system symptoms included generalised weakness and depression, profound fatigue unrelieved by rest, insomnia and difficulty in concentrating. There were occasional severe frontal headaches, but more common was a nagging occipital pain, which was pronounced when I was tired. Psychological symptoms included emotional lability and increased sensitivity to noise (I could not bear the sound of the electric polisher in the mornings). I had a special nurse who was exceptionally kind, and when she told me she was going on holiday to Ireland but did not want to go, I burst into tears, which was most unlike my usual self. I was paranoid at times and thought the staff nurse was searching my locker for tablets. Fleeting symptoms included a sharp pain in my thumb joint, and pain in the left side of my chest one night, sufficient to make me think in terms of a pulmonary embolus. The penalty of being a doctor! I first became aware of shortness of breath on lying down when I could not lie flat for a basal metabolic rate, and when convalescing I again found it was uncomfortable to lie flat sun-bathing. The muscle weakness was so severe at times that I had to ask the nurse to help me cross the small side ward (merely a couple of steps) to the washbasin where I sat down to wash. Symptoms of autonomic disturbance included temperature changes (particularly cold), profuse sweating at times, pallor and palpitations. An urticarial rash that I developed was, I think, an allergic reaction to Doriden. Muscle tenderness with occasional fibrillation was sometimes apparent.

After being in hospital for five to six weeks, I persuaded them to let me go home in an ambulance. I was so weak that I could not get up the stairs at home without resting on a chair half-way up. Convalescence was slow but uncomplicated, until the night when my mother had an attack of what I took to be anginal pain. We called in our GP and he gave her some Pethidine and said he would call again first thing in the morning. Even so, I got up to see her in the small hours of the morning when the pain recurred, and advised her to take the oral Pethidine. I could not help noticing that we both had 'the shakes'. This could easily have been put down to nerves, but I wondered why an attack of angina should produce a rigor in her. My abdominal pain was worse that night than it had ever been before and I asked our GP when he called in the morning if I could possibly take some oral Pethidine, as DF118 had had no effect. He readily agreed, bless him!

Later on that morning, we were both back in hospital, only this time in another teaching hospital. My mother had a further attack of 'the shakes' while she was in and having once pressed the bell, was unable to remove her hand from it. This did nothing to help my morale, but did confirm my view that she had a viral myocarditis, as the lassitude and weakness were far too severe for an attack of ordinary angina, and yet the ECG and enzyme tests failed to reveal the presence of an infarct.

My attacks of abdominal pain persisted and were very severe at times, particularly in the evening and the early hours of the morning. For the first time I was given oral Palfium which was very effective, but the anorexia, lassitude and muscle weakness persisted. The pain was aggravated by food, which often provoked diarrhoea with the passage of small motions and flatus. This was particularly likely if I ate fruit or anything highly seasoned or irritant, for example even a caramel sauce. I thus stuck to a bland diet and existed on fish, chicken and milk puddings. The diarrhoea alternated with absolute constipation, but unlike my previous time in hospital this was only an infrequent occurrence and did not worry me unduly.

I was in hospital for another five to six weeks while my mother was convalescing and when my legs were strong enough to go outside, I walked round and round the grounds feeling like a caged lion and very frustrated and irritable. I eventually returned home and went on a convalescent holiday before returning to general practice. This was an unmitigated disaster, probably because I was still suffering the effects of post-viral depression and did not recognise it. The little cottage that we stayed in near Eastbourne was exceptionally cold and there was no fire in the bedroom, so my breath froze in the cold night air. I always went on country walks accompanied by a newspaper so that I could put it down and sit down if I had no energy to go any farther. Even so, there were times when I looked over the fields and wondered how on earth I had come so far and how I was ever going to get back to the cottage. The more I forced myself to do, the more tired I became, and at the end far from being ready to return to work, I felt I needed a holiday to recover from the holiday.

I could hardly have said I enjoyed the break. For example, sunbathing I found was uncomfortable lying flat on my back and I had to turn on my left side. Equally, when we saw the sea, it was a major effort to scramble down the cliffs and I had to wait for my friend at the top, whilst she went down to the water's edge. All this merely served to deepen my post-viral depression, rather than lifting it. I could not return to the practice until I had got over the effects of the holiday and it was nine months after my original admission before I felt fit to do so.

My muscle weakness was still apparent in that I could not stand to lift my medical bag, but I was able to get around on visits carrying the minimum of instruments. Giving intravenous aminophylline on one occasion was extremely difficult because kneeling by the bed made me feel very shaky, but as the patient was an asthmatic, I was glad to get away with prednisone 5 mg by mouth instead. A gastroenterologist friend advised me to take no emergency calls and recommended injections of Cytamen 1000 mg. The effect appeared to be dramatic at first in giving new power and strength to my arms and legs, but unfortunately did not last.

My recovery was slow, but the symptoms gradually improved, and I was proud to be able to do a surgery and eight visits in one morning. However, a new and rather disquietening symptom appeared in the form of giddiness, though not true vertigo. I can remember driving to a friend for a weekend in the country. At every roundabout I wondered whether to turn back and the only thing that deterred me was the thought that it was farther to go back than to go on. My friend, fortunately an SRN, insisted on treating me like an invalid and really made me rest. I was dreading the drive back, but by then I felt much better and it was easier than I had imagined.

The giddiness was worse on bending and worse with my eyes shut, so that visits to church or the hairdresser became something of an ordeal. I can recall having to leave church in the middle of harvest festival services, and feeling as though I was going to faint in the middle of a perm or even a shampoo and set, especially if the hair was washed with a forward rinse which meant bending forward with my eyes shut while the hairdresser exerted pressure on the back of my head and neck. A vicious psychological circle was thus set up, with me dreading either of these two experiences and the panic reaction in itself setting up an uncontrollable fear in anticipation. I think it was also about this time that I had days when I found it extremely difficult to write and my handwriting was almost illegible.

I was back working part-time for about three months before the next relapse severe enough to entail hospital admission. This occurred in February, and lasted for two to three weeks. The pattern of symptoms forming what I called a relapse was usually the same. Sometimes I had a warning in the shape of an unexplained attack of diarrhoea, but usually the onset was insidious. Attacks consisted of severe colicky lower abdominal pain, radiating into the back, or down one or both legs. Ordinary analgesics failed to touch it, but local heat in the form of a hot water bottle sometimes helped. This was followed by profound muscular weakness, particularly affecting the legs, so that I could not stand for any length of time. Anorexia and nausea were prominent features but vomiting and palpitations were rare. I usually had difficulty in starting micturition, and my writing was difficult to read. I found it hard to concentrate or to remember people's names. Occasionally, the abdominal pain was replaced by very severe frontal headaches as the main feature, but whichever was the presenting symptom, both were followed by profound lassitude, so that I was literally exhausted after having a bath. I used this as a test to see if hospital admission was really necessary. I was frequently in bed for a week at home, but only if the accompanying malaise was such that I was afraid of passing out if I had a bath, did I call the GP in. Incidentally, after a bath, I often used to notice the cutaneous distribution of the affected nerve root was clearly mapped out. There was a distinct dividing line between the part of my leg and buttocks that was flushed with an erythematous rash and the part that was not. Venous pulsation at the wrist was another strange phenomenon. Relapses severe enough to merit hospital admission invariably occurred either in the autumn (September to October) or in the winter months (January to February). My own view was that this could be explained on the basis of intercurrent viral infections causing a recrudescence of the central nervous system symptoms.

I am handicapped in this account by the fact that I think the central nervous system damage caused by the virus I picked up (probably Coxsackie) has affected my memory and intellect. I now find mathematical sums very difficult to do, and during bad days concentration on even a lightweight book poses major problems and I find myself reading the same paragraph over and over again without taking it in. Memory loss, particularly regarding dates and times of previous admissions, I find rather trying, and I am sure that I was the despair of many a house physician or resident medical officer trying in vain to get a lucid history. Emotional changes resulted in a marked difference between 'good' and 'bad' days.

Mood swings were often sudden, varying from morning to evening like a manic depressive psychosis and I could exercise no conscious control over them.

I could never decide whether I felt unwell, could not eat and therefore felt depressed, or whether the mood change was responsible for the tiredness. I only know that I was aware of premenstrual irritability, and conversely I usually felt at my best once the period had started, so that I booked perms and so on to coincide with menstruation. On one occasion I vividly recall a National Theatre visit to Othello when I unexpectedly felt at my best, and animatedly discussed the performance afterwards with my cousin. I discovered to my surprise that my period had started a week early and I was so delighted to be feeling well that I did not mind the concomitant embarrassment. Other visits to the National Theatre and Covent Garden were not so successful. I was overcome by giddiness on a visit to Aida and did not stay beyond the first act, and a Peter Shaffer play at the National which I had looked forward to seemed as though it would never end.

I am sure readers will forgive me if from now on I just recall highlights of hospital admissions or days which stand out in my memory. In any case since the illness goes back over many years, with frequent relapses and remissions a more detailed account would be extremely boring.

One such highlight of a hospital admission was my first meeting with Dr S. I had just had a barium meal and follow-through which showed no organic lesion. However, I felt very tired and faint, presumably due to a low blood sugar because a tablespoonful of sugar which the radiographer gave me had a magical effect. My neurologist then suggested a psychiatric opinion and I was absolutely furious with her. I remember thinking that she did not believe me and thought my abdominal pain was only imagination. I dreaded a crossexamination by a psychiatrist and spent the following Saturday morning in a frenzy of apprehension. When I had had my lunch and she still had not appeared, I thought Dr D had thought better of bringing in a psychiatrist and I was delighted to have been reprieved. I was just having a cup of tea after lunch, when much to my chagrin, she appeared. Although I thought her ideas nonsensical, for example when she suggested that the nocturnal pain might be dysmenorrhoea aggravated by depression, I remember thinking that for a 'head-shrinker' she was really not too bad and much nicer than I had imagined. Subsequently, we developed a very good relationship, and many times I was grateful to Dr D for introducing me to someone who was such a source of comfort and support. At first I was acutely embarrassed at being under the department of psychiatry. I was even terrified that the taxi driver might see me entering the door. My attitude gradually changed from violent opposition to uncritical acceptance, but I hope I have now come through my period of emotional dependency to a state of unbiased objectivity.

We did not always agree, however, and when I had acute retention in hospital, I think it was aggravated if not caused by Tryptizol which had just been started; this Dr S refused to accept, largely because, quite rightly, she wanted me to continue with the drug. A swim in the cold lake at the bottom of our garden soon after leaving hospital produced excessive fatigue (I was too tired to take off my swimsuit), a feeling of faintness and a shivering attack like a rigor. I thought this was due to a hypotensive episode brought on by attempting too much too soon. I can recall thinking that I should have to go back to hospital and kicking myself for having brought this on myself. Dr S thought this was due to 'nerves' which I doubted, as I was not particularly afraid of going swimming and had tried it out before, without ill-effect.

My first severe relapse when I was readmitted to a teaching hospital involved agonisingly severe abdominal pain, which the usual analgesics simply failed to touch. Nothing stronger could be given apparently, because the registrar was unobtainable at outpatients, or so I was told. It was only by being a thorough nuisance that eventually intramuscular Pethidine was prescribed, and by then the abdominal pain had eased. But a left frontal headache had taken its place, so I accepted the injection thankfully as I felt that explanations would not help, and if I said that it was my head that was now the problem, we would be back to square one — Panadol. This was a hospital admission I never forgot, because the symptoms were as severe as the original illness.

My faith in the medical profession was somewhat shaken when I was told that I had not got a facial weakness, when I could clearly see that I had — and this was subsequently confirmed by the physiotherapist. An attack of acute retention was extremely painful since I had been encouraged to drink a lot, and for the first time I could sympathise with patients in the same predicament. The giddiness was extreme, so that I had to ask the porter to wheel me more slowly down the corridor. One acute attack occurred while I was lying in bed listening to Saturday afternoon theatre on the radio. I was desperately trying to concentrate on the play to keep my mind off the giddiness but it did not work. I simply felt that if I tried to move or turn my head even to call a nurse, I would pass out. When someone eventually came and asked me what I would like for the dizziness I was past caring, so we settled for an injection of Largactil and the attack passed off. I realised then what Dr D meant when she asked me what the giddy attacks were like and if during them I could not move even if the house was on fire. I originally thought her question was a joke, but now I saw the point of it.

Insomnia at night was not helped by otitis externa or pruritis vulvae. Muscular fibrillation was rare, but I noticed muscle tenderness, particularly of the Achilles tendon, when I was being blanket bathed. An aching pain at the back of my neck was worse when I was feeling tired, and another annoying, although not disabling, symptom was coldness of the legs, particularly marked when I was sitting up. Enemas or even suppositories were apt to provoke a recurrence of the abdominal pain and when this was severe at night, accompanied by extreme thirst, it ended up for a reason I could never fathom with irritation of the tip of the nose. Profuse sweating occurred at times, although I was afebrile and I gathered my temperature, far from being raised, was usually subnormal.

When I left hospital, various symptoms came and went. Blurring of vision in the surgery one morning made the prescription pads swim before my eyes and I could not focus sufficiently to write for about 30 minutes. Facial ache resembling toothache or trigeminal neuralgia came and went, as did a tremor of the right hand. This was most noticeable first thing in the morning, when I was putting on lipstick or trying to write. It was also worse when I was tired, such as at the end of a surgery or clinic session. Taking blood for an ESR was alright, but measuring the right amount into the specimen bottle was another matter. Delicate manoeuvres such as vaccination, or filling up an injection showed the tremor more markedly. I could resort to subterfuge for the latter by turning my back on the patients or asking the mother of a young patient to wait outside while I drew up the injection. But I did not know what nervous mothers and babies would think if a doctor with an obviously shaky hand gave their child its vaccination. When I tried an anti-Parkinsonian drug one weekend it made me feel dizzy and I was afraid of dropping the best china while drying up.

The symptoms of the illness itself were so bizarre that when trying any new medication, it was impossible to tell which were side-effects of the drug and which were manifestations of the illness. Giddiness, for example, was no new thing for me, particularly on bending or getting up suddenly, and there were mornings when I felt it would be unsafe to lock the toilet door. Tiredness and the impossibility of standing for any length of time were the two most disabling symptoms. I was so tired some mornings with a busy surgery that I rang for the secretary to get the thermometer from the washbasin, because I felt too exhausted to cross the room again. She often had to write up the notes for me as well as my handwriting by that stage had become illegible.

Friends would sometimes comment on my pallor, and the possibility of jaundice or malabsorption occasionally crossed my mind when the urine was dark in the mornings and accompanied by diarrhoea with pale frothy stools. I developed a distaste for fried foods and alcohol and could not face rich things like cream or chocolate. Nor could I face strawberries or bananas, which had formerly been great favourites. I found I had subconsciously adopted a low-residue diet — when the hospital dietician suggested this and showed me the diet sheet I found I already instinctively avoided the foods contraindicated, even preferring milk to plain chocolate.

'Bad' days at home usually involved lower abdominal pain. One such attack was particularly severe, and the colicky pain felt like dysmenorrhoea. I felt sick, my mouth was dry and I sweated profusely. I counted the minutes until our GP arrived at 4 in the morning. I apologised profusely, but fortunately he was very kind and gave me an injection of Pethidine. On another occasion I had to call him in for symptoms resembling intestinal obstruction. Again, the lower abdominal pain was severe and colicky and I was being sick about every 30 minutes, which was most unusual for me. I took several analgesics with no effect at all, and even an injection of Largactil failed to affect the vomiting. This was followed by a week or more of absolute constipation. On another occasion, I was violently sick before I could reach the bathroom, and although the abdominal pain was less severe than usual, I was relieved when the doctor called the next day and assured me there were no physical signs of intestinal obstruction.

The attacks of pain usually started with lower abdominal discomfort, then built up to a severe colic, which ended with a neuritic pain like sciatica radiating down the right or left leg or both and sometimes into the back. This sometimes ended in myalgic pains in the right upper arm or face. In the early stages a hot water bottle eased the abdominal discomfort, but when the pain reached the neuritic stage, nothing, even oral Palfium or Pethidine seemed to diminish it. Fortunately, this stage did not seem to last as long as the abdominal one.

During my next admission I was given a course of eight ECT treatments. They certainly helped the abdominal pain, possibly by breaking the circuit of conditioned reflex which had been set up. Although I had two bad attacks in hospital before the treatment was completed, I did not have any after returning home. My memory was not helped although it slowly improved. I found I could not remember the clothes I had in my wardrobe, my physiotherapist's name, or the way to Lambeth Hospital's hydrotherapy department (although I had been there several times previously). The ECT one morning followed a night of severe pain and when the anaesthetist asked routinely if the injection was comfortable, I said the anaesthetic was sheer bliss.

My recollections of this admission are somewhat muddled and confused. For example, I remember friends visiting me or nurses being kind, but have no idea of what they said. My sense of dates and times (never good at the best of times) was made worse, and I had no idea of how long I had spent in hospital; I still have to look in my diary if anyone asks me. The effect of adding Marplan in the morning and Surmontil at night seemed to make my confusion worse. I felt lightheaded and drunk on more than one occasion and positively paranoid on others when I thought the other visitors and patients were staring at me or Sister disliked me. During my weekends at home, in my confused state, I was terrified of adding cheese to a white sauce without thinking. Whenever I felt faint or dizzy, I became positively hypochondriacal, wondering which article of food I had mistakenly eaten.

The ECT and vigorous physiotherapy for the muscle weakness undoubtedly helped. I had my doubts about the anti-depressant drugs however, when these seemed to aggravate a pre-existing tremor of the right hand, and made writing letters or even cheques almost impossible. Although I felt much better, and wanted to try driving, I felt it was inadvisable while I was still so shaky.

Shortly after leaving hospital, I went to an Albert Hall Prom. when one of my favourite works was being played. The whole arena seemed unreal and when the music started I still felt giddy and had to focus on the carnation buttonhole of the man in front rather than watch the orchestra conductor, in an attempt to keep my balance by concentration. We had to leave at the interval, but I thought it was due to 'nerves', and not being used to crowds of people. I therefore went out a few days later to a conference at the Royal College of General Practitioners. This was even worse because during the first two lectures, I kept feeling as though I was going to faint and fall to the right. I was glad the place was full of doctors and the one on the right looked strong enough to prevent me falling to the floor. Needless to say it did not happen, but I could not eat much lunch and had difficulty carrying a drink without upsetting it. When I steeled myself to ask a question later in the day, it was embarrassing to find that my left leg and my hand were trembling violently.

A less severe attack of giddiness occurred when I went out to the shops with my father. I felt that I had to remain seated in the car and would pass out if I moved and I had to let him do the errands for me. A symptom I had not noticed before was reluctance to cross the few planks which bridged the stream at the end of our lake; I felt the bridge was too narrow and I might fall in.

I think the anti-depressant drugs aggravated a pre-existing tendency to fluid retention; the abdominal distension was more marked, urinary output less and bras and corsets felt too tight. This culminated in an attack of acute retention in which the pain was as severe as in any attack of dysmenorrhoea. Catheterisation was avoided by only a hair's breadth. Reducing the Surmontil tablets made me realise how much better I felt on them, so I gradually restarted them and hoped constipation and acute retention would not recur. In this, as in the amount of walking, I felt a delicate balance had to be struck. A certain amount of gradually increasing exercise was obviously beneficial, but too much would result in exhaustion and a recurrence of the depression.

Whilst in hospital, pruritis vulvae often aggravated insomnia and following the episode of acute retention, I was advised to see a gynaecologist. This seemed a good idea as my periods were irregular with a tendency to menorrhagia and I was slightly worried by a brownish-red intermenstrual vaginal discharge, which was worse during relapses. All was well, however; the gynaecologist diagnosed atrophic vaginitis and advised me to repeat a course of oestrogens for three months. At first I thought these were causing nausea and morning sickness, but I soon realised that this could not be so, as it made no difference if I stopped them.

Thirst and a craving for sugar allied to pruritis vulvae suggested the possibility of diabetes to me. I had had two glucose tolerance tests during my previous admissions, which were slightly abnormal but not markedly so. It was a senior registrar at a teaching hospital who first told me of the relationship between the central nervous system and the skin which explained a number of otherwise baffling symptoms.

I would conclude with some reflections on how to sustain the morale of patients with a long, debilitating illness and the eternal question of whether or not to tell them the truth. As a doctor, the truth hit me during my first severe relapse, when the patient next to me with a facial paralysis told me that she had looked at her notes and found she had a virus infection of the central nervous system. This was confirmed by her husband, who had been told that her illness was incurable. As the registrar took her history, I could not help realising how much it resembled mine, even to the extent of being asked if the morning headache was worse on 'lying in' in bed on Sunday mornings. I realised then with a shock that my illness behaved like multiple sclerosis, but whenever I mentioned this to anyone I was continually fobbed off with the reply 'you only think that because you are a doctor and are imagining the worst'. One registrar even went so far as to say that there was nothing wrong with my nervous system, even though he had himself written in the notes 'recent memory poor', which I gather is a symptom of organic disturbance. When I said I could not write properly because of tremor in my right hand, he said it was due to writer's cramp. I am doubtful whether this would satisfy the least intelligent patient, and certainly not a doctor. This type of reaction only serves to destroy what little confidence the patient has left in his doctor. We often tell patients the truth only when it has become unavoidable and by then the damage has been done and the vital bond between doctor and patient has been damaged beyond repair. I am convinced it is due to moral cowardice on our part that we cannot bear to be truthful and the kinder the neurologist, the worse his dilemma. However, if patients ask their doctors for the truth, I am sure they should be told, although it may not be the most appropriate time for telling them. Only then can they start to come to terms with their situation and learn to accept it.

This account is taken from the chapter entitled 'Encephalomyelitis' in *Sick Doctors* edited by Raymond Greene and published in 1971. With the advantage of hindsight, it is possible to realise that not all of the symptoms described, in particular the abdominal pain, were due to ME. A subsequent operation revealed acute intestinal obstruction, with many adhesions surrounding the site of the original appendix operation, and a right-sided ovarian cyst was also present. When the obstruction was relieved and both ovaries and uterus later removed, the symptoms improved dramatically, confirming the diagnosis of endometriosis and adhesions.

My last two relapses were sheer hell because of the combination of physical and psychological symptoms and the lack of understanding by the nursing staff, who were totally unfamiliar with the syndrome and failed to realise that rest in the acute stage is of paramount importance. My present symptoms are physical weakness and muscle fatiguability so that I am exhausted, for instance, by the preparation of a meal, and on 'bad' days cannot even take a bath. My leg muscles are weak, so that my walking distance is restricted and I have to use a stick. I cannot stand in a queue for a bus or in a supermarket. Shopping expeditions have had to be abruptly curtailed when I have had to stand around waiting to be served. I frequently felt so faint while shopping that I had to sit down, and on one occasion I even had to ask a stranger for a lift back to the car. If I have one of these fainting attacks I find that food revives me, even if it is only a cup of sweetened tea.

Mood and muscle weakness vary from day to day and from morning to evening. On 'bad' days I can hardly talk coherently on the phone. I forget people's names and places and cannot remember what I was about to say next. If a correspondent says 'put it in writing' my heart sinks as I cannot type even a short letter without drafting it first and typing an article or letter on a 'bad' day seems beyond my wildest dreams. As 'bad' days outnumber 'good' by about two to one, it is difficult to book theatre tickets or plan holidays in advance, because you never know how you will feel at the time. Giddiness and fatiguability make it impossible to drive except locally. I find I cannot make up my mind in a hurry and on 'bad' days, even find it difficult to decide when to cross the street. I cannot carry heavy shopping or lift a weekend case, however lightly laden.

A minor but annoying symptom is coldness of the legs, so however unfashionable it may be I nearly always live in trousers. If I try to dress up and wear court shoes, my walking distance is even more restricted. Another annoyance is that I cannot attend a whole-day conference sitting in an upright chair (particularly if there is no support for the back) without getting an aching pain in the bottom of my spine, which has been sufficiently bad on some occasions to make me leave a lecture. I also get an aching pain in the back of my neck if I am sitting for a long time and this is worse when tired and limits my neck movements when driving.

Unlike multiple sclerosis, ME has encephalitic features such as loss of memory, concentration and depression that in some ways make it even harder to bear. I apologise for the discursive nature of this article, but as the illness has been with me now for approximately 20 years, it is difficult to remember events in their right chronological order.

Editor's Note

This account of her illness by a doctor-patient lists all the typical symptoms, but is complicated by gynaecological problems (a not uncommon complication), which led to surgery on two occasions. I think it likely that the initial admission for appendicectomy was due to a viral appendicitis, since she had a raised white blood cell count and a subacutely inflamed appendix. The prolonged recovery is typical of ME.

CASE HISTORY 4

J.G.

When my illness started in July 1978, I was working as a nursing sister in the casualty department of Preston Royal Infirmary. I was very fit and active with an excellent health record of only four days sick leave in 18 years.

I developed 'flu-like' symptoms one weekend, rested for a day and returned to work on the Monday. A week later, I wakened one morning with a very enlarged gland in my groin. I went to work and was examined by a medical registrar who referred me to the consultant surgeon who was puzzled and thought he should excise it. This was never done as the swelling began slowly to subside. During this process I felt ill and toxic but was on holiday for a week, so was able to rest. I did not have any treatment.

On returning to work, I felt unwell most of the time, with headaches, dizziness and staggering. Three weeks later I parked my car in the town centre and as I went to collect a ticket I suddenly felt as though I was going to die. The feeling came over me suddenly and I did not feel as though I would get home. After a couple of days in bed, I again returned to work (there were already a number of members of staff off sick with 'flu') but during the next few weeks I felt worse and worse, until finally I had to consult my GP and stay at home. Antibiotics and tonics were prescribed without any effect, and then I developed hypertension following local anaesthetic for dental treatment. Anti-hypertensive drugs were recommended but my blood pressure could not be controlled.

In November, when I was sitting in a chair watching television, I suffered what felt to me like a coronary spasm. My head felt queer, I became cold and sweaty and again thought I was going to die. The ambulance was called and I was taken into hospital, where blood tests, ECG, EEG, lumbar puncture and X-rays were done. As these were all normal, it was deemed psychological, which was devastating because I felt so ill. Following my discharge from hospital, I developed angina, extreme fatigue, arthralgia and my spine felt rigid and very painful. I was prescribed anti-inflammatory drugs which aggravated my circulatory problems and made me feel worse.

80

After a second stay in the hospital with no improvement, my GP referred me to a medical specialist in Hope Hospital, Salford, who really tried to help me during my five periods as an inpatient and several visits as an outpatient. Many different types of medication were tried without any significant result; some of them, I felt, made me worse. I suffered further episodes of circulatory spasms, hypertension, tingling, myalgia, abnormal bruising, fatigue, unsteady gait, mood swings, extreme pallor, sleep disturbance, angina, cold extremities, visual disturbance and a poisoned feeling. For a period of a few weeks I felt some improvement while taking a course of Vibramycin. Unfortunately, this was short-lived when again following local anaesthetic for dental treatment, I quickly went downhill and felt absolutely dreadful.

My last stay in that hospital was soul-destroying because once more, as I did not fit into a certain category and most of the routine tests were normal, it was decided that my illness was psychological rather than organic. I felt completely demoralised — here I was with a nice home, loving husband and family, a job which I enjoyed, everything to live for in fact, finding it very difficult to live through the misery, pain and uncertainty of each day. More than a year after my illness began, I was bedridden, feeling worse, with no hope.

My husband, who never gave up throughout, contacted Northwick Park Hospital, Harrow, and following a consultation with Dr Raftery, the cardiologist, I was admitted for a stay of eight weeks for intense tests and observation mainly of a cardiac nature, but everything was done very conscientiously and with great skill and interest. I regained my confidence and was certain the answer would be found. Sure enough, Dr Hillus-Smith from the Royal Free Hospital, who had been called in to give an opinion, said I was suffering from ME. After that I was also found to have a heart irregularity and advised to take cardiac medication. Was I seeing daylight at the end of the tunnel? I went home full of hope, only to find that I was having problems with the medication. The dose was adjusted, but still I felt worse taking it. Why was this? No-one could explain. The medication had to be stopped!

I tried to find out more about the disease now that I knew it's name, and in doing so made contact with Dr Ramsay who was interested enough to get myself and two colleagues, who had similar symptomatology, admitted to Coppetts Wood Hospital where, following tests, my diagnosis was confirmed and the other two diagnosed for the first time. Where did I go from here? Still feeling really ill, unable to live a normal life or to work, no cure or hope of a cure in the near future, and suffering from a disease that doctors did not understand or believe in. Almost two years passed by. All my original symptoms were still present, plus the fact that I felt more 'poisoned' after food and I had an enlarged liver.

I carefully noted everything I ate and how it affected me and realised that ordinary foods like apples, fish, bread, and so on which I had always eaten without problems, were now causing trouble. If I took a simple headache tablet or vitamin supplement I became really ill. For the third and final time I had some local anaesthetic and the angina, muscle weakness and fatigue, was worse than it had ever been. Back in Northwick Park Hospital with a different team of doctors who were unable to understand my problem, I was again labelled neurotic and sent home. I decided that I would have to fight this thing myself.

I read the two books by Dr Richard Mackarness entitled *Not All in the Mind*, and *Chemical Victims*. This was the start of an unbelievable chain of events. I experimented daily with various diets until it became apparent that all foods except potatoes and brown rice affected me. In sheer desperation, I stuck rigidly to these two foods, plus drinks of hot water for a few weeks; nothing else, and no tablets of any description. I improved significantly. The pain in my spine which had been severe and constant for more than two years, disappeared; the angina which was so bad that at times I felt I was being strangled, disappeared; I felt brighter, clearer and had more energy; the tingling, numbness and headaches improved. I was greatly relieved, but didn't know how I could continue to live on such a diet.

I decided to take Piriton tablets to see if I could counteract the allergies. I collapsed with terrible vertigo and vomited for days and had to lie motionless in bed and found it difficult to walk for quite some time. Who was going to help me now? It had to be a clinical ecologist.

From the very first visit to Dr Monro's clinic for desensitisation treatment, I began to improve. The treatment is not straightforward and requires a lot of will power and patience to carry out, but the rewards have made it all worthwhile. Not only was I affected by foods, but all kinds of chemicals and even the chlorine in my drinking water. All of these things have had to be dealt with. Soon after starting the treatment which enabled me to have a better diet and helped me to cope with all the pollution in the atmosphere and so on, I was able to return to work, initially on a very part-time basis. I have gained weight (and am now back to normal) and can feel quite well and relatively symptom-free provided I do not veer from my diet at any time. The smell of paint or a couple of liquorice allsorts can bring about a relapse and anything containing vitamin C triggers an attack of angina and painful joints.

Why most doctors are unable to understand this immunological problem is beyond me and I feel very sorry for the many people who are suffering badly and not receiving the sort of help they really require.

Editor's Note

This is a very interesting story with a happy ending because since writing it, after two years of treatment, the patient has been able to dispense with all her desensitisation therapy and has been able to resume her work full-time as a casualty sister. She is able to live the sort of life she never dreamt would be possible again. She still has to avoid food additives and preservatives which can produce giddiness, tremor and tingling in the head and down one side of her face, and if she eats anything with sugar in it, such as honey, it brings back the fatigue. She now has any dental treatment needed without a local anaesthetic. Incidentally, the symptom of feeling as though 'I was about to die' is a not uncommon part of the ME syndrome.

CASE HISTORY 5

J.A.P.

It was September 1968 when my wife became ill with what we thought was the usual influenza virus, which lasted three weeks. During this period she was more often than not suffering from fainting spells. As my wife began to recover, I went down with this so-called flu. But by the third week I had begun to lose the use of the right side of my body, plus the sight in my right eye. (*No* blood tests were taken.)

I was admitted to Romford Old Church Hospital for a series of tests and it was diagnosed that I had encephalitis and this had left me with epileptic seizures. This I would not accept. I fought my hardest to overcome the illness and was able to return to work after six months, but on returning to my place of employment I could not cope with the responsible position I held as material controller. My pride would not accept this and I left and took a semi-skilled job and seemed to cope quite well, as long as I had long periods of rest. This meant that we had to adjust our lives to a limited social life. If we had a late night out, I would have to sleep most of the next day to recover for work the following day. During this time, my wife took on more and more responsibility and on my advice began taking driving lessons, with which she found it hard to persevere. Having been a very active person I did not adapt too well to the restrictions my illness had imposed.

Perhaps I was wrong in not returning to my GP to inform him of the side-effects I had been left with. Zooming or flashing lights would trigger off numbness, a pins-and-needles sensation in my right arm and leg, speech impediment, fatigue and debility. If I lost my temper or quarrelled at all, I would suffer the above symptoms and feel extremely ill for days. I had to learn greater control over my emotions.

Whilst I was undergoing tests at Romford Old Church Hospital, I was unfortunate enough to see a young lad in his teens (on the opposite side of the ward) who had also suffered from an unknown virus infection, which had left him paralysed down one side of his body and during the short time I was there, he underwent another two operations which left him worse off than before. Can you wonder that I did not wish to return? His virus and mine may have had nothing in common, but I did not think rationally at that point in time.

As the years rolled by, our sons were growing up and acquiring vehicles of their own and I would insist on helping them with their car maintenance as well as my own. Even though my wife insisted that I was overdoing it, I became determinedly obstinate and refused to listen. I even ignored the warning sign, which was strangely enough the smell of carbolic, which usually meant ease up. In September 1977, my wife and I had worked extremely hard on our eldest son's wedding reception and the following month I felt so ill from fatigue, side blindness in my right eye again, pains in the head, stiffness at the back of the neck, continually dropping items and having difficulty in writing even my own signature (my hand would not obey my commands), that I could not work. After four months it was suggested that I return to my job as a process operator in charge of two deburring machines, on a part-time basis. I found a lack of understanding in my place of employment and I was pressurised into coping with full-time output in part-time hours. The pressure became so great that I had to return to full-time employment for my own survival. I managed to keep going for almost another year, with the tiredness ever increasing.

In January 1979, I entered Honey Lane Hospital for further investigation. It was one doctor's opinion that there was some damage to the central nervous system — just an opinion, not proven. I returned to my job. Then suddenly I had an attack of vertigo, whereby if I moved my head even slightly I would vomit. (This is now controlled by drugs.) To avoid bumping into doors, door frames or objects in my path, I have to deliberately misjudge the distance and (if I'm not distracted) this technique works. I cannot stand for any length of time without feeling ill and faint. To overcome this, I have a folding seat and it also acts as a walking stick support. It is the only means I have of getting out and about (in areas where one cannot take a car) and without my folding seat I could not cope. This illness has left me totally reliant on others as I can no longer drive myself. I agreed to a course of psychiatric treatment, but didn't care too much for the heavy drugs. But whilst I was attending day therapy, I realised that those with mental problems were far worse off than me, which gave me an entirely new outlook on life in general.

In October 1981 I suddenly lost over two stones in weight, which coincided with a burning sensation in the middle of my spine. I cannot bear pressure or touch on that area of my spine. I also suffered with bowel problems for the first time in many, many years. At times I have spasmodic tremblings in my legs and arms. Spine X-rays revealed nothing abnormal.

My wife says that I cannot always follow conversations and often give wrong answers. But her own description of this illness is likened to a rapid ageing process. On my good days I do wood carving; I've learnt not to try on my bad days. I have had to accept that anything I attempt will never be perfect since I have had the misfortune to catch this menacing virus infection, or whatever else it might be. But I am fortunate enough to have an understanding and caring doctor, to whom I shall always feel grateful.

Editor's Note

Typical points in this case history are spasmodic trembling in the arms and legs and inability to stand.

CASE HISTORY 6

N.P.

It wasn't until I was 32 and a third-year student nurse that I discovered that I had ME, although I probably contracted the disease at the age of 14. Periodically through my teens I suffered bouts of malaise, muscle pains and above all, lethargy. I felt 'flu-ish' but never had a raised temperature. My symptoms were usually worse in the mornings and evenings, and when I was overtired or under stress. At that time I underwent extensive medical investigations, but nothing abnormal was revealed. I learned to almost disregard these episodes and, indeed, they occurred quite infrequently.

The first winter after I was married the symptoms started to recur with depressing regularity — every two or three weeks. I put it down to 'picking up bugs', although I seldom suffer from colds or flu. The next year the same thing happened and I sought medical advice. The symptoms seemed so nebulous that my doctor couldn't take them seriously, and tried giving me iron pills, advice on a nourishing diet, and reassurance; all without success. I was working as a medical secretary at the time and often had sick leave, which made me feel guilty and frustrated, as losing one's employer's confidence adds to the stress and strain of a chronic illness. I asked my doctor to refer me to the hospital where I worked, and again went through a series of blood tests, a searching history-taking and even a psychiatric consultation. Once more, nothing abnormal was found, except that it was thought I had had glandular fever. I was advised that, following this illness, recurrences are common and that they would disappear in time.

I still believed this when I started training as a nurse. I enjoyed the training immensely, and expected to feel more tired than the other students on account of my age and the fact that I had a home to run at the same time. I did well in my training, and worked and studied hard, but after a while the gruelling life began to take its toll of my health. My relapses became more frequent and, in my ignorance, I tried to battle on. When this was impossible and I simply couldn't work, I told lies to my employers, and even to my GP. I claimed to have a migraine, or flu. I simply couldn't let on that I had a recurring vague illness that had no name. I began to turn inward and wonder if I was neurotic. Relatives and friends considered me 'sickly', and 'always picking up things', and once or twice even suggested that my symptoms were a subconscious way of opting out of life for a few days every now and then.

One day, during a bad spell, I poured out all my problems to a doctor at the hospital. Surprisingly he was sympathetic and suggested a consultant to whom my GP could refer me. Surprisingly again, my GP also took me seriously and off I went for my consultation. The consultant heard my story, and a smile of recognition appeared on his face as he told me I seemed to be a classic case of ME. I had never heard of this disease but to be told I was classic and not a freak did wonders for my morale. He told me that, as yet, little was known about ME and there was no cure available, and advised me to get adequate rest and not to allow anyone, not even myself, to consider me a hypochondriac or a malingerer. He suggested that I try to modify my lifestyle by trial and error; the most effective means a sufferer has of controlling the disease. In the evening when my husband came home I was a comic sight, grinnning from ear to ear, and saying cheerfully that I had a recognisable disease! The psychological effect of that consultation changed my life, as I could now look the world in the face and start to accept my problem.

My next good fortune was hearing about the ME Association, which I joined immediately. The comfort of knowing there are others similarly placed to oneself is enormous, and here was a chance to become involved in publicity and promotion of research. I 'came clean' at work and found that one of the nursing officers knew of the disease as she had witnessed at first hand the Royal Free outbreak in 1955. She took me under her wing from then on — supporting me when I wanted to work through one of my milder relapses, and firmly insisting that I take time off when I was clearly too ill to work. To qualify was my aim, and I did it largely with her support.

My husband has always been a tower of strength to me. He understands that I am a person who needs to achieve but, like the nursing officer, he knows when to make me stop. Then he quietly takes over the running of the home and allows me to rest. Family and friends of sufferers have a lot to contend with, as it's hard to accept that a person who seems to be brimming over with health and enthusiasm one day becomes pale, weak and quiet the next. I never hide my condition from people, but think if wiser to explain why I don't like long walks and too many late nights. On the other hand, I do not encourage people to look upon me with pity or treat me as an invalid, since for quite a lot of the time I can carry on normal activities, and I feel that a person who constantly fusses over themselves soon loses appeal.

I am now working as a part-time staff nurse. As my employers are aware of my health problem, they do their best to ensure that I don't work on very heavy wards. I should have liked to further my career by doing my midwifery training, but I know that this would jeopardise my health, and I am very pleased to have at least achieved my ambition of becoming a qualified nurse.

My health has improved now that there is less pressure in my life. When off duty I try and rest for a while each day, and if I feel unwell I simply shelve the housework for a day or two. I have a little dog and manage to take him for walks in the park, although I confess that I drive him there and back! I feel optimistic about the future. Hopefully, ME will become well known to the public and the medical profession, and a cure may be found for us all. I may even enrol for that midwifery course one day.

Editor's Note

This account too, describes a typical history.

CASE HISTORY 7

E.S.

I first became ill in 1963, when I was 39 and lecturing in zoology at the London University. In December, I had what appeared to be an attack of mumps, but after three days I found that I could not walk properly, and was exhausted. My feet were cold from my ankles to my toes; it felt as though they were encased in cold socks. I was very shaky and could not control my temperature.

When muscle pain started in the legs, I was taken into King's College Hospital, but nothing abnormal was discovered. As soon as I rested, I felt better. But throughout the following summer I became increasingly tired. There was no weakness of the arms, only a slight pain. But I did have tightness and a constricting feeling in my throat and upper chest, and sometimes a definite pain. I got weak and dizzy before meals, and was found to have a low blood sugar, particularly in the mornings. The symptoms were intermittent; one minute I could not walk as far as my car, or the length of a train, or climb stairs, but then in hospital, once I had rested, I could run up stairs with ease.

Not surprisingly they concluded in Queen's Square (a specialist neurological centre) that my illness must be psychological. I was forced to give up my job in London and moved to Swansea, where I worked part-time, but could organise my lecturing to fit in with my afternoon rest. Even so, I had a long relapse from 1971 to 1974, during which I began to realise that my symptoms — although inter-mittent — did seem to be worse after meals. In 1977 I went to the Bencard allergy clinic, but they could not find anything wrong. I had no strong family history of allergy(apart from one aunt who had an allergy to make-up) but later I found I was allergic to chalkdust and make-up products containing perfume. Both of these allergies were contracted while I was teaching in Nigeria for five years.

I began to investigate my eating habits. In 1979 I cut out dairy products altogether and felt a lot better. Then, in September 1979, through a friend and fellow sufferer, I heard about an allergy clinic run by Dr John Mansfield. I started treatment with him in January 1980. He found that I was allergic to 13 foods. The most important were dairy products and all cereals; then came chocolates, coffee, grapes and yeast. I took sub-lingual drops for two years, and there was a remarkable improvement. But if I forgot to take the drops and ate even a cheese straw I suffered a very violent reaction.

Now, after the treatment, I can eat anything, except products containing wheat flour and pills containing calcium carbonate. I am virtually cured, unless I come under stress or get over-tired. The inability to co-ordinate my legs seems to be related to an allergy to cheese; chocolates cause tingling in the legs; milk makes me feel nauseated and very tired and oats make me depressed. A diagnosis of Royal Free Disease was made in 1965 by the neurologist Dr Reginald Kelly, and later confirmed by my own GP — two years after the onset.

Editor's Note

This patient is one of the sufferers from the ME syndrome who has been helped by treatment for allergies. Some patients do remarkably well on this treatment, but it is not always possible to predict in advance which patients will benefit. She is now very much better and has stopped taking the drops. She remains allergic to wheat and milk and has had maintenance enzyme-potentiated desensitization treatment at increasing intervals, now down to once a year. On this regime she has stayed very well and apart from needing an hour's rest after lunch each day she can now walk and do most things.

CASE HISTORY 8

G.E., Aged 25

I was 19 when my illness started. I went to Germany in 1976 with my local Youth Orchestra, as a principal trumpet player. By the time I came home, I had lost a lot of weight. I had a blood test for glandular fever which was negative, so I was told my illness would eventually pass. But it did not and I spent another ten days flat on my back running a high fever.

It is interesting to note that another girl on the German trip was also taken ill at the same time and thought to have had encephalitis — unhappily my diagnosis was not so easily made. I resumed my work at College learning the piano and the trumpet, but throughout that year I had pains in the head and felt generally weak. I noticed a restriction in my breathing towards the end of the term, and could not produce my best notes. I passed all my exams, except that for the trumpet which was too physically exhausting for me to take.

I went to a specialist neurological hospital at the end of the first year, when I had some sick leave. The significant symptom now was that my right shoulder was drooping; it was seizing up like a frozen shoulder. I was told it was a kind of frozen shoulder which would go in three weeks' time, but I noticed that my other muscles also tended to go into a kind of reverse action; when I tried to contract my leg, I would push the foot down instead of bringing it up.

The hospital suddenly decided they were going to use hypnosis instead of more orthodox treatment, because there was nothing they could find wrong on neurological examination. They did an IQ test while I was still heavily sedated and said I was not clever enough to be a musician. They hypnotised me in a little room and then made me walk up and down the ward, while the hypnotist supported me just with his right arm. The worst damage to my morale was done when he told me that I would never make a top-class musician. The hypnosis did me no good and made me self-conscious, because although the hypnotist told me my movements were better after the treatment, the other patients in the ward told me there was little difference. At one point, a social worker made an offhand remark to the doctor which greatly frightened me; she said 'What happens if the spine fuses?'. I was discharged home, because after nine weeks in hospital I was no better and asked to be allowed out. One doctor at the hospital said 'I know you are not well enough to be going home, but what can I do about it?'.

When I came out of hospital, I tried an osteopath for a time, but gradually my condition deteriorated. I found it difficult to walk and bent lower and lower until I had to use a wheelchair. While my parents were away I went right off my food and experienced generalised muscle pain. My parents then arranged a private appointment to see a rheumatologist at a teaching hospital. But ten days before the appointment I had acupuncture treatment to the base of the spine and by the weekend I had developed a fever of 104°; an emergency doctor was called, who said I should be admitted to hospital straight away. Next day I was very ill and another emergency doctor said it was an infection of the waterworks and gave me antibiotics.

I was eventually admitted to hospital and the rheumatologist there was going to do a lumbar puncture, but suddenly changed his mind. I was referred to a neurologist who vetoed all neurological investigations and put me on sedation. At one point another patient's husband phoned my father at 10 p.m. because I had turned a ghastly colour and apparently coughed up blood. While I was in the rheumatology ward, I was allowed home for weekends, but I was so weak that I fell out of my wheelchair on one occasion. But towards the end of my stay in the unit they had found high titres of Coxsackie virus in my blood stream. When I came out on Valium, Distalgesic and Pyridoxine I was very ill, panting for breath and I could not control jerking movements of my neck; it was as though I was drugged.

I then saw a homeopathic doctor and went to the Ladbroke Clinic to have a complete physical check-up. The only abnormal finding was the possibility that I had a gastric ulcer and a high titre to measles virus. A neurologist from another specialist hospital then saw me and said I had had encephalitis. He kept me in for three days and shortly after I was sent home after physiotherapy, and did in fact start to walk. I was fairly well until I went on holiday to Clacton, which left me feeling weak. Later, when I went away again to the same place in hot weather, I found it was much more of an effort to try to walk.

I went away again to a caravan, this time in Dorset. While there, I was slightly irrational and when I went to Bournemouth one day my walking became weaker and weaker and I got closer and closer to the ground. Friends suggested a walking stick, but I was reluctant to start using one. I could not enjoy the sun either; sitting out on the patio, my face became bloated and swollen, and since then I have had quite severe reactions to sunlight. I could no longer walk because my left leg had become so weak, and the only way I could get about was by using one leg and a walking stick. When I got home, I was hospitalised again for another two weeks and then a rehabilitation centre was suggested. At that stage I could just about walk with crutches, but my left leg was dragging along the ground. The specialist then retracted his encephalitis theory and said it was psychological. After three months at a rehabilitation centre I was no better and since then my illness has got progressively worse.

Eventually, I landed up under a neurologist in a specialist unit at Glasgow, and the diagnosis of ME was at last made.

Looking back, the illness probably started when my shoulder became weak in 1976. Since then, I have had typical symptoms of ME; muscle twitching, spontaneous bruising at various times, pain throughout my muscles and tender focal points. The pain has only occasionally been bad enough to keep me awake at night, but I have had difficulty getting off to sleep and often wake up early. I get depressed, have puffiness under the eyes and have 'good' and 'bad' days. Symptoms are sometimes worse in the morning, sometimes in the evening, but they are invariably worse premenstrually. The periods are very heavy, but not painful and I have twice been incontinent of urine, I think as a result of waiting too long. Two glucose tolerance tests carried out during the last hospital visit were both abnormal. Sometimes I feel hyperactive, but more often I feel faint and sweating and on such occasions sugar at once revives me. I could not write for a long time and have difficulty in remembering names and cannot always find the right words. With headaches I sometimes get blurring of vision, and cannot stand bright lights. On bad days, I have a 'ghastly pallor' and it feels as though my eyes are swollen. Occasionally I have jerky neck movements, which can be a bit embarrassing.

Editor's Note

This patient untypically has had a very acute illness with gradual deterioration. She is now confined to a wheelchair and can only sit up with difficulty. Her left arm has become wasted and her neck muscles are also weak. Unfortunately, the generally unsympathetic attitude of her neurologists has persisted and she has been labelled 'conversion hysteria' by more than one hospital which has only served to increase her mental anguish. Recently, however, the sympathetic attitude of a medical consultant at another hospital has dramatically changed the picture. She is now receiving physio-therapy and occupational therapy daily on an outpatient basis and is able to bathe herself, sit up and be transferred by car instead of ambulance for her treatment. She has also been able to play the trumpet again and, in spite of a continuing low-grade fever and severe headaches from time to time, her morale is greatly improved.

CASE HISTORY 9

Doctor S.D.

In the week before my twenty ninth birthday, a physician at the Royal Homeopathic Hospital in London diagnosed ME. As I had gone to the hospital expecting to be told that my symptoms were due to tension, anxiety, stress or chronic depression, his assessment totally stunned me. During the days that followed, I carefully considered what he had told me, and the distinct possibility that he might be wrong. My doubts were fuelled by the fact that no one had been able to identify a specific physical abnormality during all the years I'd been ill. Moreover, the notion of a physical illness which could be so disabling, yet exist for years without any clinically detectable signs, seemed a little far-fetched. At the same time, the psychiatrists and psychotherapists whom I had consulted had also based their diagnoses on what I had told them, not on the results of a disease-specific laboratory test.

In fact, there have only been three occasions during my life when any recordable abnormalities were found. The first of these was identified when I was nine. On the basis of the findings, my GP diagnosed acute rheumatic fever, overturning his previous opinion that my mother worried too much and that my aching limbs were typical growing pains. The second abnormality was discovered when I was 18, having gone to the doctor complaining of tiredness, and feeling as though I had the flu. This time, the GP was able to confirm what he had suspected all along, namely that I had succumbed to glandular fever. With a smile, he told me to keep off the alcohol for the next six months, and as a footnote, warned me that I might continue to feel tired for several weeks.

Unfortunately, the tiredness continued for well over a year, and what's more, my misery was exacerbated by frequent attacks of angina in my throat. After 18 months of antibiotics, gargling and foul tasting lozenges, the GP referred me for psychiatric assessment. The psychiatrist sat behind his desk and asked me a lot of questions about my youth and my parents. He listened attentively and seemed very sympathetic, until I mentioned how my problems seemed to worsen after I'd contracted glandular fever, at which point, to my astonishment, he stated that I had never suffered from that illness. Convinced that my memory could be trusted, I replied that I'd spent a week at the health centre during my first year at university, and that the GP had based his diagnosis on the results of a blood test. However, before I could finish what I wanted to say, he stood up, walked towards me and repeated that I had not suffered from glandular fever. He had spoken to the GP and read my notes. I was lying. Utterly confused, I left the room. The psychiatrist had prescribed a course of tablets, which made me feel pleasantly woozy and seemed to lessen the severity of the symptoms. They also made me feel totally indifferent to what had happened during the previous 18 months and I ceased to care whether I got better or not.

My introduction to Valium also coincided with the cessation of my visits to the GP. Not only because he'd turned me into a liar, but also because he hadn't been able to help me. I had sensed for several months that I'd been labelled a neurotic nuisance, so I approached the student counsellor for advice. My life as a student had been dominated for over two years by the need to conserve my limited energy, and I had missed a lot of lectures. It was a miserable time. Whenever I felt well, I spent virtually all my waking hours trying to catch up with my work, and there was little time for extracurricular activities. I felt lonely, frustrated and above all, envious of my fellow students' ability to combine their studies with various social activities. Fortunately, things improved during the third year, and to everyone's surprise, I passed my exams with flying colours.

With renewed confidence I embarked on a postgraduate course at the University of Amsterdam, but I remember several occasions when I was forced to stop what I was doing because I felt tired, giddy and even seasick. This was most annoying, especially when I was working with patients, but I usually coped with the aid of glucose tablets and ordinary anti-histamine preparations. I was seeing a psychologist at the time and although she kept most of her thoughts to herself, I became convinced that my lapses, as I called them, were just due to anxiety.

At the end of my fifth year at university, I relapsed once more. However, this time I was able to report a respectably high temper-ature which remained fairly constant for 10 days. It seemed incon-ceivable that my blood tests wouldn't show any abnormality, but that's exactly what happened. So both my GP and I shrugged it off as a rather atypical bout of flu, but when my post-flu tiredness was still bothering me two months later, I began to despair. By this time,

I'd seen two psychologists and two psychiatrists for my 'nerves', and my GP refused to send me to another. Instead I was sent to the swimming baths and told to eat plenty of vegetables. The swimming made me feel worse and I had to drag myself to the shops. My whole body felt so weak that I often wondered what was keeping me up. Queueing at the check-out in shops was particularly unpleasant. Standing made me feel faint and light-headed and there were never any seats on which to rest so I slumped over the trolley, trying to keep the weight off my feet and pretended to be studying what I had bought.

Again, I took about 18 months to recover, but this time, the recovery was not complete. I contracted one dose of sinusitis after another, and I began to experience acute attacks of nausea. Complete strangers commented on my ghostly pallor, and asked me if I was feeling all right. Ever since I had started to feel a little tired, when I was still a teenager, I tried to keep my symptoms to myself. I suppose I could have told people that I was just suffering from anxiety but I feared rejection and ridicule, so whenever possible I made up a plausible excuse, and prayed that the problems would disappear.

Having obtained my degree, I realised that I would not be able to do a job which involved a lot of standing and walking. As I enjoyed working with people I decided to train to be a psychotherapist. But history repeated itself, and halfway through the two-year course, I relapsed again. I went to the health centre, told the physician that I had suffered from flu for the past month or two, and waited. She told me that flu didn't usually last more than a week and that I looked both anxious and stressed. I left with a huge bottle of Valium and finished the course. My supervisor advised me to carry on, but I felt that it was irresponsible to treat patients when you couldn't give them your undivided attention, so I left university and went to see the professor of psychiatry.

Although my temperature had been above normal for some weeks, the blood tests showed no sign of infection. So I became a psychiatric outpatient, and underwent a number of tests. When I asked what these tests had shown, the psychiatrist refused to tell me. His successor was a woman and I hoped that she would be more sympathetic. Unfortunately, she was even more unhelpful and insisted that I was wrong in thinking that a diagnosis had been made in the first place.

During my training, I'd learned that you couldn't begin therapy without having made a comprehensive assessment first, and that you had to make at least a provisional diagnosis before deciding what type of help would benefit the patient. As she had decided on the type of therapy which would suit my needs, I assumed that a provisional diagnosis had been made. In order to resolve the confusion, I made a formal application to examine the contents of my medical file. The whole procedure took two years, and when I was eventually handed the file, it became obvious that much of the contents had been removed. Nevertheless, what was left made interesting reading. According to the psychiatrists, I was a hysterical personality, suffering from conversion symptoms. These symptoms were my way of attracting attention. With a diagnosis like that, I wasn't surprised that they'd been so unfriendly and distant. I also discovered that the psychiatrist whom I'd consulted when suffering from sore throats, had reached a similar conclusion. Nowhere in my notes could I find a reference to glandular fever or of my stay at the health centre.

By this time, the symptoms had become chronic. I found myself another psychotherapist, underwent more tests, and was pleasantly surprised when she admitted to being baffled. When I told her what her colleagues had diagnosed, she laughed. Both she and the psychiatrist who was attached to the clinic, suspected that there was something physically wrong, though neither of them knew where to begin looking. Then one day, the psychotherapist, called Anneke, suggested that I should experiment with my diet. A dietician gave me an exclusion diet and my blood was tested for signs of food allergy. To my amazement, both revealed that I was allergic to milk products. It was only the third time that I'd been able to show a doctor that there was actually something wrong with me. I wrote a letter to the GP who had diagnosed glandular fever, asking him how he had arrived at that diagnosis. In his letter, he confirmed the diagnosis, adding that the blood tests had demonstrated the presence of antibodies to the Epstein-Barr virus. I felt exonerated!

Anneke had encouraged me to go back to work and after some hesitation, I started lecturing and counselling. However, by the time Anneke and I had gone our separate ways, I was feeling worse than ever. A few minutes of cycling triggered an acute attack of nausea, which abated as soon as I rested. I'd begun to dribble, my speech was often slurred and I noticed tremors in my arms. Some of my students thought that I was an alcoholic, as, unable to keep my balance, I often swayed in front of the blackboard. And on top of everything else, I'd started to experience extremely severe facial pains for which no cause could be found.

As soon as I had found suitable therapists to take over from me, I left clinical work to concentrate on writing. Reading and writing were my passion. But after about 15 minutes, I started feeling sick and my head began to feel heavy. It was as though my brain had been in a spin-drier and even after I stopped reading, the inside of my head felt as though it was rotting inside my skull. When I lay down, I could feel parts of my body swaying, some to the left, others to the right. And when I stood, I felt the ground underneath swaying like the waves of the sea. Eventually, even watching television triggered these phenomena so when I wanted to see a particular programme, I spent most of the time listening with my eyes shut. Then last year, I started to feel light-headed and unsteady while standing under the shower. Having assumed for many years that the bulk of my problems could be explained as manifestations of anxiety, I was confronted with a symptom which I couldn't incorporate into this neat little theory. I panicked and phoned Anneke. She came to see me and recommended that I went to stay with my parents in London. Then I remembered an article I'd found in a woman's magazine, which mentioned an illness characterised by exhaustion. I'd read some of the scientific literature on this illness during my years at university, but at the time I hadn't recognised its relevance to me. Nevertheless, I showed the article to Anneke, and later to a neurologist, and both told me that it would be worth following up.

Many months later, I phoned a member of the Surrey branch of the ME Association. She asked me what my symptoms were, and when I told her, she seemed to recognise all of them. It was the first time in ten years that I didn't feel like a freak. Meanwhile, my old GP had retired and his replacement believed in the power of the mind over matter. At first, he was sceptical of my illness, but after he had seen me several times, he agreed to refer me for special tests. The consultant studied the literature and I was admitted to hospital.

This proved to be a complete waste of time as all the test results were normal, leading the consultant to speculate that the symptoms were probably the result of *suggestion!* When I returned to London, the family doctor sent the community psychiatrist to see me at home. He noted that I seemed depressed, inferring that this was the core of the problem. When I tried to discuss the factors which in my view had led to the present difficulties, he looked quite blank. He advised me to walk as much as possible and to ignore the literature on ME. There was in his opinion, no way in which a virus could cause the kind of symptoms that I was experiencing.

The next psychiatrist also asked a lot of questions about my upbringing and my relationship with my parents, concluding that I was very distressed and would benefit from an intensive long-term course of psychoanalysis. I explained to him that I couldn't afford it and that the idea itself didn't appeal to me. He dismissed all my arguments, contending that my training allowed me to manipulate those who were trying to help me. In other words, he believed that I had tried to hoodwink him and his predecessors. Trying not to cry, I confessed that my education had enabled me to focus on and evaluate my feelings more deeply, but that my aim had been to give honest answers. For I knew all to well that it was counterproductive to deceive the therapist. It would be me who would suffer in the long-run. I couldn't deny that psychological factors were involved, but I wasn't convinced that they were the primary source of my symptoms. Finally he suggested that perhaps I didn't want to get better. His remark didn't surprise me; one of his predecessors had left me with the same thought on which to ponder.

Back home I considered my options. I could barely walk or stand and there were few distractions. I was limited in the amount I could read and I was becoming increasingly more isolated. It was Jenny from the ME Association who pointed out that I had to see someone who understood ME, and persuaded me to visit the ME clinic in London. Since then I have been to see another psychiatrist, who only spent 20 minutes with me, but in that time showed a great deal of empathy and understanding. Unlike many of his colleagues, he thought it was perfectly plausible that my symptoms could have originated from a viral infection and he asked me to try a concoction of drugs which he thought might help. Unfortunately, it didn't.

Epilogue

In a perfect world a psychiatric diagnosis shouldn't relegate the sufferer to the status of a second-class patient. But this isn't a perfect world and in general, a patient with a broken leg can expect much more sympathy and understanding than the patient with a broken heart. To the majority of people, mental illness is an unknown quantity. There's no plaster of Paris cast or sling for others to see;

there are no scars to prove that there is something wrong. People find it difficult to assess the suffering of the depressed and anxious, and therefore to empathise with them. A person whose distress is mediated by psychological factors often has to convince others that he or she is genuinely unwell, and not putting it on. Most people I know, including my GP, think that my symptoms are largely 'all in the mind' and think that I should 'snap out of it'. Convincing them that I can't has been very hard work. None of them seems to know what it is like to feel permanently exhausted and at the end of your tether. They only have their own experience with which to compare mine, and this is possibly the reason why one of the most common pieces of advice I've come across is to pull myself together. I know people usually mean well, but in my opinion, the latter is more of a dismissal than a constructive and helpful comment.

Sadly, many of those who should know better hold the same attitudes to mental illness as the population in general. They, too, have a tendency to blame the victim for his or her predicament, believing that many patients are either using their symptoms to gain attention, or simply dealing with their personal problems in the wrong way. As a result, they may appear uncaring and distant, lest showing sympathy should encourage the sufferer to continue complaining. Having peculiar symptoms also compelled some psychiatrists to approach me as they would a naughty child and I soon began to yearn for someone who would treat me as an adult, an equal. Not surprisingly, most of the doctors were somewhat reluctant to discuss the diagnosis with me and few allowed me a say in the management of my illness. Had I suffered from a recognised somatic condition, life would surely have been easier.

If my experience is anything to go by, people who develop symptoms which cannot be evaluated and confirmed by clinical tests have many battles to win. They have to fight against the trivialisation of their distress; they have to fight against the myths which surround chronic illness, especially the widely held belief that illness is a way to attract attention. But, most of all, sufferers have to fight against widespread prejudice; while this prevails, they will almost certainly remain second-class patients.

Editor's Note

This is an interesting history and all too common in that vague symptoms of fatigue and depression have been attributed to a psychological rather than a physical illness, although there was a clear history in this case of glandular fever preceding the onset of ill health. The difficulty in standing is absolutely diagnostic and other typical symptoms are 'sea sickness', giddiness and tremors in the limbs. It is also interesting that the patient's 'faint feelings' could be helped by a tablet of glucose and that her 'ghastly pallor' was commented on by colleagues.

CASE HISTORY 10

J.C.; Illness Began Age 35

I have always considered myself extremely lucky in this life: born to loving, outgoing, full-of-fun parents; surrounded by friends of all ages and a younger brother I had always wanted. School was great, especially the sport and social side, and I proceeded to qualify as a physical education specialist, on which I had set my heart. I contracted all the usual childish ailments — except mumps — including scarlet fever and German measles several times, I was told. Yet I hardly missed a day's school, or later a day's college, and seemed to have boundless energy.

In 1965 I married and continued full-time teaching, running a Church dance drama group, teaching in Junior Church, coaching tennis and examining swimming, besides sitting on nine committees and caring for my husband and two small boys. We were a blissfully happy and healthy family until 1972, when my older boy, three and half years old, was sick during our summer holiday. A few weeks later he was unwell again and couldn't seem to recover, although our GP could find nothing wrong. My once bouncing boy would lie on the ground crying and staring into space for no apparent reason and was no longer keen on his play group. Then both sons developed a throat infection and high temperature which for my younger caused a convulsion and a hospital stay. Our GP decided both boys should be tested for epilepsy; thankfully the results were negative.

My younger son returned home from hospital and slept and slept. My older boy could not sleep, waking at 2 a.m. and crying till 5 a.m., holding his tummy and head alternately, and yet too young to describe how he felt; still our GP could find nothing. When my younger one eventually woke up fully several months later, he appeared quite better. His happy, clown-like personality returned, except for occasional aching in his legs and back when he was tired. My older son, who was not thought to be unwell so had not been put to bed, remained quite languid, dreamy and often pale. For him school began, and I remember his teachers saying that he had a good academic brain, but why did he sit down in the playground and go to

104

sleep on his desk? Was he anaemic? Once again I took him to our GP, pleading for something to help him sleep at night but 'He is perfectly healthy' I was told; so our little boy struggled on, by now irritable, petulant and tearful, which is not his true personality. It really hurt to watch him suffer every day and I spent most nights by his bed rubbing the back of his head upwards where there was often a soft swelling. This was where he put my hand and it was the only thing that would lull him to sleep.

At the end of 1973 I was aware of a strange pain in my groin and then in 1974, after a knock on my right breast, of a pain which wouldn't go away. The back of my skull had a tender spot, exactly the same place as my son's, I had ear ache and the top of my right arm felt permanently bruised. I was tired, but was extremely busy with my teaching, committees and family. I remember bursting into tears when with a friend who was helping me to organise Christian Aid collections in May, which astounded her and me, I felt indefinably unwell, yet couldn't pinpoint how, except for the aches. I played badly in a tennis match, feeling sick after the second game, and discovered my temperature was 99.6 when I returned home. This temperature became my norm, between 99.2 and 99.8 everyday. My husband persuaded me to go to our GP, who suggested I visit a cancer clinic to have a check up; thankfully all was clear, but I still felt unwell and I now felt that my GP thought I was exaggerating not only about the children but also about myself. Whilst I was taking 96 children for a Royal Life Saving examination in an outdoor pool my voice completely disappeared, although I felt no worse. It was nearing the end of term and I was needed to organise the sports day, and so on, so I couldn't stay away.

At last holiday time came and with my voice renewed we were off to Devon. Whilst I was making the bed before a planned day on the beach with our enlarged family of energetic relatives and friends, the room reeled and I could do nothing but collapse on the bed feeling sick and indescribably ill. I lay there, wondering what had hit me; I felt as though I couldn't move. To me, this is the moment my illness began, although I hadn't been fully fit for the past year. I slept the holiday away. My worried husband insisted that I visit a Devon doctor, who examined me thoroughly, saying there were three sets of glands up and it could be glandular fever, but nothing could be done if it were, so there was no point taking a blood test — just rest.

Next term I felt rotten, but recovered enought to take on an 'O'

Level Human Biology class as well as my usual subjects. By dropping as many evening activities as possible I staggered on at school, taking my babe with me and finishing in time to meet my big boy from school. Gradually my body became worse and my temperature began to fluctuate wildly, ranging from 95.6–101°F. Strangely, when it was high I felt I could cope, but suddenly it would drop rapidly, as though it could fight no longer and my whole body seemed to be packing up. Between lessons I found an empty room where I lay flat on the floor, often in tears, to recover enough to get through the next 40 minutes. My GP took blood tests for glandular fever and found my white cell count high, but that was all — nothing to worry about and no mention of stopping work. I now felt nervous of visiting my GP as he never found anything wrong; how could he understand that the suffering was real? Each evening I tucked up the boys and then fell into bed myself, having given up all evening activities. Just two weeks before the end of term I fell when catching someone vaulting over the box and I knew I couldn't go on; I felt as though I were in a permanent stupor. I slept for two weeks and roused myself for the usual Christmas efforts. I kept a temperature chart which fascinated my GP; it still ranged from 95.6–100°F. I tried to explain to him that I felt unwell all the time but that suddenly I would feel drained and desperately ill, as though I was fighting to stay alive, which must have sounded very exaggerated, but wasn't, and at that time my temperature was always low. He listened, but it obviously meant nothing to him, so I was sent to a Guy's Hospital specialist.

At Guy's they took 35 blood tests; X-rayed my chest, abdomen and skull; took EEGs and ECGs; all were normal. As this well-known specialist could find nothing except a low-grade fever, as he called it, he firmly suggested I saw a psychiatrist — much against my will. The psychiatrist delved into my past and present, but could find nothing abnormal. He seemed positively pleased when I said my sexual appetite had increased! He decided it must be masked depression, for which he gave me some anti-depressant tablets. Sent home, I dutifully took these, but after the second dose I really thought my heart was going to stop. My temperature dropped from 99.8 to 95.2°F in under an hour and although I still thought of myself as strong, the notion that I could die was very real and very frightening — not that I fear death but I feared dying at the hands of those who had meant to help me. There was disbelief from my GP — all his tests showed how healthy I was — but I was re-admitted to

Guy's, and first my mother and then my husband were interviewed by the psychiatrist. I wrestled with the thought that they were trying to prove it was all caused by some deep seated worry from the past; I didn't feel depressed, only frustrated and ill. I wasn't used to being disbelieved. I lay there waiting for the result of these interviews like a prisoner awaiting sentence.

To my delight, I had 'psychologically impeccable' written on my form, which I wanted to pin up over my bed. My lovely Mum and gorgeous husband must have said all the right things: but suppose I hadn't had a fulfilled childhood and hadn't been happily married, would I have been put back on those awful tablets and my physical symptoms ignored? I listened while at the foot of my bed each doctor said I didn't belong with them; the psychiatrist was certain it was a medical problem and the medical specialist was certain it must be psychological. So I was sent home with 'post-viral syndrome' written on my discharge form. I was assured it would clear up within two years. It was a relief to leave the hospital where the reality of my symptoms was disbelieved, where I was not allowed to sleep enough and was chivvied into going for little walks to improve my weakened muscles and to eat sitting up with the others. Social talk was as great an effort and as exhausting to my head as standing or walking was for my body.

By now my legs and back ached as well as my arms, neck, head, ears and eyes. I had suddenly become photophobic, especially with artificial light, and I preferred the curtains drawn and no light switched on over my head at night. I thankfully welcomed my parents who moved in to take over the children and I just slept 23 out of 24 hours for weeks on end. I was roused for meals, which I forced down, crawled on hands and knees to the bathroom and back, and just managed to give a kiss, cuddle and prayer to the boys each night as they climbed on my bed. Even to talk was an effort, or to open an eye or move a painful limb, but I felt peaceful and surrounded by love; the anger I felt at the hospital melted away. All life seemed an enormous effort and I had a desperate longing for deep sleep. There seemed to be no improvement and my husband began planning a downstairs bedroom, as the stairs were impossible. I felt palpitations alternating with extreme slowness of heart beat, for apparently no reason; there was a build-up of extreme pain at the base of my skull and top of my arms and rib cage, with the occasional twitching muscle in the leg or shoulder blade. My vision was as if in a dream, grey and difficult to focus; I had ear ache with nothing to show for it and an overpowering weak and ill sensation. This was the daily pattern for several months.

I firmly believe that if I had been chivvied at this stage of the illness and not had my husband's understanding and my mother's and father's devoted care, my system would not have recovered at all and I would have been bed-bound for life. I believe I should have died from heart failure and no-one would have realised that it was actually caused by this post-viral syndrome because all tests would have proved negative. I was numbed when the phone rang and a familiar voice told me that a mutual friend of ours with ME, my age and about as ill as myself, had had a tooth extraction and died, not recovering from the anaesthetic. Although in recent months her doctor had said that her heart was perfectly good, her death certificate said 'heart failure'.

That summer a young girl, Helene, from France came to help me; she stayed a month. Two days before returning she felt unwell and tearful and subsequent letters from France spoke of continuing up-and-down health, but the doctors could find nothing wrong and thought it was all psychological.

Our two boys' school reports were concerned by their frequent absences and by the older boy who was lethargic, disinterested and lacking in confidence. The younger one was dynamic for a period and then would collapse and be brought home, or the phone would ring and we would be asked to fetch him. He would sleep for two or three days, complaining of leg and back aches or abdominal pain, but once over this, he was bouncing again, for a while at least. Our GP, examining our younger boy's abdomen whilst he was crying and rolling on the bed with pain, commented that 'of course, a child would pick up symptoms if there was illness around him', and dismissed any further examination or help. He seemed to have forgotten that they had symptoms before mine.

This dismissal was hard to take and was then followed by the suggestion that the boys might be better at boarding school. If he had wanted to sap any last vestige of my self-confidence he couldn't have chosen a better way to do it. Gra and I ached for our boys who became extremely despondent with life at times because they were unwell so frequently. Work was becoming a pressure so were the games though they basically loved them. Straining to go to school when unwell meant eventually a longer time away to recuperate, then back to catching up on work missed, which seemed to create further illness. Tiredness and strange aches and pains seemed a weak excuse as their reason for absence notes. I longed for someone medical to say it was right to keep them at home, that it was a phase they were going through and it wouldn't last. Or that their health and happiness had to be restored before formal education could be at all beneficial. About now, although my memory for exactness of timing could well be wrong, I became covered in red spots from head to toe — presumably German measles again, but I wouldn't let Gra call our GP. I felt too frail to face another encounter and anyway, if anything I felt better with the spots than I did usually.

The encounter that made me resolve never again to ask for medical help for myself if I could possibly avoid it took place two years later when I was supposed to be better, and was to a certain extent. Occasionally when well enough I took a friend for tennis coaching, sitting on a stool in our garden and throwing balls over the net. Afterwards I walked up the steep incline to the house feeling gradually more and more unwell, sat down and was hit again by excruciating pains, especially in my chest and arms. I felt faint with a terrible malaise and sudden exhaustion, as though the cork from my energy bottle had been removed and life was draining away. Rather than cry out I instinctively remembered the prenatal exercise of deep breathing when in pain. This I did, but I couldn't stop without immense effort of concentration and Gra rang our GP. He arrived and by then I was calm but still in pain. Instead of helping me understand why I had been in such pain and suggesting what I should have done, he was irritated with me for hyperventilating, telling me it was this that had caused the pain, not the other way round, and wanted to inject me with some sort of tranquilliser. I refused, which further annoyed him. I slept for a week or two had a summer holiday and then as advised prepared to teach again for two hours twice a week.

In the meantime, a friend told me of a BBC Woman's Hour broadcast by Dr Celia Wookey she had heard, speaking of a strange illness that sounded like mine. I wrote in and to my delight was sent a questionnaire asking about symptoms which the medical profession hadn't wanted to hear. This was the beginning of our ME Association in which I readily became involved and for which I am ever grateful to Dr Wookey. A name to describe abnormal behaviour is somehow much more acceptable to the general public than to admit one doesn't know why one is staggering as though drunk or whatever the illness decides to do to one.

I knew I wasn't well but I was advised that going back to work would be a good rehabilitation. I saw my family off to school and work, then climbed back into bed, sleeping until half an hour before I was due to catch the train. We had to sell my car as we were without my earnings and had to find two lots of school fees. I managed and enjoyed my two hours teaching but the journey home and the next few days were murder, with renewed aches and pains, nausea and seasick giddiness. After a netball lesson I walked along the corridor to the foot of the stairs leading to the staff room and I knew I couldn't climb them. My body slid down the wall to the floor and, looking at my watch, I realised that the corridor would be full of feet in one minute's time, when they changed classes. So aching all over, I crawled into the games cupboard under the stairs just as the bell sounded. The geography master noticed my rear end disappearing, so crawled in after me to see if he could help. This made a lovely spectacle for the passing children but also my weakness was now known.

This caused another problem for me. Our head revealed that several parents were concerned that I might be infectious and, what did I think? This was a blow; I already had a friend that feared to visit me and I really could understand her fear. However, I had been told that my illness was only infectious at the beginning and my teaching was all out of doors, so my conscience was clear, although doubts were raised and I felt the emotional pangs that lepers must have felt. Also I was getting worse daily and, quite suddenly, it hit me again full blast and I could hardly move. My temperature went mad and I felt as bad as I had two years earlier. About ten days after my relapse my husband and both boys developed a rash on their elbows and knees. The boys were both unwell with their own particular symptoms; the older one with headaches, eye aches, and tummy pains and the younger with aching legs, back and abdomen and red-rimmed eyes; both also with sore throats and no energy. My husband was fine at the time but shortly after he carried our sleeping younger son upstairs after driving to Devon for Christmas. His legs ached by morning and he felt generally unwell. We both lay in bed rather helpless but my recovery was beginning. Doctor friends who knew about my illness suggested a blood test. Two and a half weeks had passed and I was well enough to drive home, for Gra was far too weak to do more than climb downstairs into the car. For the first time I was more capable than he, although I still felt ill. The journey was hard. I kept stopping every few miles to sleep and gain strength for the next few. The blood tests were phoned through; abnormal with a creatine phosphokinase of 2,700, but our GP said 'Probably all flu tests would be like that'. So nothing was done and Gra fell ill and became slowly worse. One day a shout from the bedroom called me to find he had fallen backwards whilst sitting on the bed with a tray full of lunch and he couldn't sit up. He had in one month changed from a 13 stone, fit, sporty, weight-lifting lover to a weak and painful, helpless heap. The two boys still weren't well and I felt awful — but whom could we turn to? I wouldn't ask friends as by now I was scared that I really was infectious when at my worst. No one seemed to believe us — it was a nightmare.

I asked a virologist friend to ring the virologist at our local hospital, the one who had dealt with Gra's creatine phosphokinase level and ask him to phone our GP and get him to do something for Gra. My arms were so painful I was in tears most of the day as I tried to cook meals and carry them upstairs, lying down every few minutes to recover enough to continue, and just helplessly watch my husband get worse. At last our GP returned with someone to give a second opinion, a neurologist from the hospital. He listened to my husband, who now found it hard to talk or eat as his throat had swollen so much. It became plain to me that this man was not taking Gra's symptoms at all seriously. Our GP had obviously told him of my plight and this was jeopardising help for Gra. Although I was standing there he said to Gra, 'How does this so-called Royal Free illness affect your wife?' 'She feels exhausted, her arms are painful', he answered. The specialist turned, walked towards me and said, 'You mustn't allow imaginary illnesses to get you down — you look perfectly healthy to me', and with that he playfully slapped me on the arm. It hurt and I was already so angry that I blindly struck out sideways, hitting him hard on the chest and sending him reeling. 'I think I had better go', he said with as much dignity as he could muster, and I heard my GP apologising for me all the way downstairs.

I wasn't proud of my action and I didn't like what was happening to my personality but it was the culmination of anger that had built up over the years of disbelief. However, it was this meeting that seemed to change our GP's mind. On the phone this consultant suggested that I was psychologically ill but I heard my doctor disagree. At this I felt a wave of trust return. Memories of us both banging our fists on his desk in the frustration of argument diminished and he tried to reassure me of his belief in the illness; sadly, though, there is still some healing required to dissolve the defensiveness between us and renew proper communication. Again, this illustrates the importance of understanding this illness at its start which would help so much to preserve the doctor/patient relationship. However, he then sent another specialist to us and after this, and a frantic call from me saying Gra could hardly swallow at all, Gra was admitted on a Sunday as an emergency patient to hospital. He was carried downstairs to the ambulance with his whole body seemingly swollen. He was given a muscle biopsy and told he had polymyositis, then dermatomyositis, and given a large dose of steroids, which immediately began to work, although he still had to be fed with slops in order to swallow.

I seemed to feel tearful all the time and permanently exhausted, trying to shop and cope at home. I was collapsing more frequently and never felt well, although some parts of the day were better than others. I visited Gra every day but continually had to stop the car and lie back to rest after every mile or so. The steering wheel was too heavy and my legs and arms hurt too much and my tears blinded me. I wasn't crying because of anything specific, I was just so exhausted and every movement was such a painful effort that I couldn't stop crying, but it was embarrassing because I still looked very fit. I can remember saying to myself over and over again, 'if only I can keep moving I'll be all right.'

You see, if I woke stiff, aching, with sick pains (if it wasn't a bad day when I'd collapse before reaching the bathroom) I can honestly say that if I slowly got my circulation moving and made myself get up, the stiffness and aching cleared and pain subsided. The trouble is that it was then tempting, as I did in the beginning, to push myself on and imagined that movement was actually the cure. Always when I did stop, the symptoms became slowly worse, building up to a climax about half an hour after my circulation had slowed down. Yet if I pushed myself on when the floating colourless world and growing exhaustion told me to stop, determination and muscular strength could keep me going — for a while at least. Of course when I did stop, the pains — and worse than that, the frightening indescribable malaise that deprived me even of my true personality, and left instead an unreal world where communicating with my closest ones required an enormous effort of concentration — overpowered my strongest will.

The longer I pushed myself on, the longer the really bad time lasted. At my worst the effort of lifting a drink to my lips or speaking one coherent sentence was too great and occasionally I felt I had lost the use of my right arm, especially in bed where I used my left arm to prop my right on pillows to ease the pain. Sitting gave little relief; I needed to lie flat and wait for the climax of pain to pass before complete relaxation produced a healing calm. Then the day came when I couldn't drive, so the boys couldn't go to school and as I lay on the landing I told them to find the bread and bring it up so I could cut them something, but we ended by pulling the loaf apart and eating it dry. The boys got their own food and had to help me back on to the bed.

I felt thoroughly useless and, if I was ever depressed, it was at that moment, letting both my husband and boys down, with nowhere to turn, and because of my fear of being infectious not wanting anyone in the house. At this stage I also found it hard to sleep and hard to pray. My body seemed like lead, yet my brain seemed to have an unceasing motor which refused to rest, thus making sleep impossible. Small noises were like an electric shock to my system, even the click of a switch. The anger I still felt for the unnecessary extra suffering Gra had endured through lack of action and belief from the medical profession inhibited my ability to pray and know God's presence. When eventually I confessed this anger toward all those who refused to understand my boys, my husband and myself, I could pray again and then of course I was at peace, so could sleep again. Deep sleep, 12–15 hours out of 24, helped me back to coping, so by the time Gra came home I could manage the essentials except the shopping. It was standing that made shopping the worst of all the chores. Gra, thank goodness, was better and by autumn term he was lecturing again.

At the beginning of 1979 eighteen of us were sent to Glasgow. Dr Peter Behan gave us numerous tests, ECG, EEG, lumbar puncture, the 'needle shocks' (an electomyogram I think), more blood tests and the eye and brain one where they linked my scalp to a machine while I watched some flashing lights on a sort of chess board. This hurt my eyes and made me feel extra sick, but I was kindly treated and this meant a lot. I was able to take Dr Behan's pounding out of questions and answer him back with relative calm because of his genuine concern. It was a comparative haven at that hospital because those in charge actually believed me. Dr Behan was very interested that Gra was diagnosed with dermatomyositis at the time of my severe relapse.

The journey to Glasgow and the tests made me weaker and iller and I shall never forget the total disorientation I felt as a good friend led me through the station to catch the train home. It was morning and this is often the worst time of the day, especially if I have to sit still or stand. I felt as if my legs were heavy and yet jelly-like and my body was bruised all over as though hit by small hammers. I felt poisoned, my head was out of control, and so were the tears — no balance, seasickness, nausea, my eyes refusing to focus and my ears and eyes telling me I couldn't bear the noise and movement of that station for another moment. It passed, as these awful times do.

A friend I met at Glasgow with ME who has been 80 per cent bed-bound since her lumbar puncture said something that has haunted me, 'Generally people only face death once in a lifetime — but with this illness I go through the sensation of dying so often.' Her family has split up because of the illness; she is still struggling to find a meaning to life lying in a darkened room for the majority of her time feeling ill. She has my deepest admiration.

One day I received the letter from Glasgow and listened while my GP read out that they had actually found some abnormalities. My gratitude for Dr Behan's persistent belief in us amidst doubting colleagues was quite overwhelming. I was so enthralled, excited and exhilarated that my confidence fully returned and has never again left me. How vital it is to have a diagnostic test for the peace of mind of all who suffer this wretched illness. The letter said:

> No physical or neurological abnormalities were found but a definite elevation of I.D.H. The cerebrospinal fluid was abnormal with the presence of oligoclonal bands and a marked elevated beta 1 band in the CSF. Abnormalities in phasic grouping on routine electromyography and conspicuous abnormalities in jitter on single fibre E.M.G. An increase in the serum IgM with a marked depression and barely detectable serum IgA. There were positive autoantibodies for gastric parietal cells but the intrinsic factor was normal. A decrease was found in C1Q and C4. The above information suggests but does not prove that this patient is suffering from a persistent virus infection.

This, of course, was not a diagnostic test, but it satisfied me, I now had the confidence to fight for my children. All they needed was to be able to be away from school whenever they had to, without being chivvied. A friend introduced me to Dr Michael Dillon, a doctor from Great Ormond Street Children's Hospital, who was sympathetic to this illness and offered to see the boys in his own time, for which I am deeply grateful. He said, of course, that he could not diagnose them, but that their symptoms made them likely sufferers. So he wrote to their schools asking that they should not be pressurised in any way, mentally or physically. Since then both boys have learned to pace themselves, staying away from school for the odd day when they need to rather than pushing themselves on until they are really ill and are away for a week or longer before recovering. Both now are practically 100 per cent, although neither as yet has as much stamina as the majority of their friends, and if overworked or overtired their own particular symptoms once again reappear. My husband is definitely 100 per cent now, but his illness took a different form — his muscle cells completely broke down; his creatine phosphokinase level was high and the steroids helped him. One specialist is certain that we all had the same viral attack but our bodies reacted differently; another is doubtful.

Someone I must mention at this point and who I wish I had known at the start of the illness is Dr Melvin Ramsay, President of the ME Association. From the moment I met him, his positive, directive approach was a source of strength and guidance to our family. He wasn't afraid to risk his reputation and would talk or write to anyone about his beliefs concerning ME. He even bothered to telephone our GP, visited Gra when he was ill and lead a prayer group at our home. It seems to me that he is a pioneer of holistic medicine in the true sense of the word.

Then ten ME patients were sent for a myoglobin test because an acquaintance of ours had found that our muscle cells had become semi-permeable and he believed that when we used them they leaked myoglobin (the smallest molecule in the cell) out into the blood stream. After the first test I was fascinated because my count was the highest at 840, the norm being 10–70. A woman far worse than I, who was taken there in a wheelchair, read only 730 — of course her count was taken without her moving, whereas I had bused and jog-trotted into the hospital. I was sorry that the research stopped there. Only one blood sample was taken but the subsequent publication *Post Graduate Medical Journal* (1979 vol. 55, p. 856) referred to a supposed second test. This mystified me and I still haven't had any explanation!

It was exciting to broadcast on BBC Woman's Hour with Dr Wookey, in 1980 (although I had to lie flat on Broadcasting House floor for half an hour beforehand) pleading the case for ME. It was rewarding to know we received over 1,000 letters from interested

parties and undiagnosed sufferers. Then later that year, news
arrived to say that the Association could receive charitable status.
To me we had achieved our first major goal, and at this stage I
retired from the central committee to concentrate on the Surrey
Group, and recover from all the travel and emotional battles.

A holiday in France brought an underlying horror of mine to
reality. We arrived to learn that two days earlier Helene had died.
Sometimes her throat had swelled and on this occasion she had
panicked and had choked to death. On her death certificate was
written 'heart failure' because they could find nothing specially
wrong with her throat or any other part of her body. This tragedy
really knocked me over and I was flooded with guilt and enormous
grief. Listening to the description of her suffering I recognised so
many of her ailments and although I'd been worried and had sent
some ME literature for her to take to her GP it had been dismissed.
She was labelled as incapable of coping with life and her symptoms
imagined; yet it seemed that these imaginary symptoms actually
killed her. This lovely 21-year-old girl died suffering alone when I'm
sure an individual understanding her illness could have helped her
through to recovery.

In 1981 I attended a Christian faith healing meeting led by Trevor
Dearing. Nothing special happened except the build-up of pain,
sickness and brain deadening from sitting too long although I
warmed to him and loved the atmosphere he created, until he told
us to empty ourselves to allow God to take over. Although I'd heard
this challenge before, it now took on a new meaning, but I couldn't
do it. My mind was full of 'ifs' and a friend practically dragged me to
the front where Trevor Dearing laid his hands on my head. He
began speaking, then stopped, shook my head vigorously but
gently, saying 'Let go — you must let go'. At this point I must have,
because I suddenly collapsed and apparently lay on the floor for 20
minutes in a waking stupor. At the end of the service Trevor
Dearing came round my side of the church, shook my hand and
asked how I was. 'I feel a hypocrite', I said, 'I often collapse on the
floor and I still feel ill'. He looked at me steadily and smiled. 'You
are no hypocrite, you were on God's operating table a long time;
healing could take as long as a week. Don't analyse, just accept;
leave it to God, go home and forget it.' He left me feeling relieved,
and I was led shakily to the car.

It was the following Tuesday, as I was climbing out of the bath,
that I realised I had done so without aching or giddiness. I stood on

the bath mat and knew it had happened: there was a warm glow all through my body, with an ecstatic feeling of closeness to God that I sometimes feel after a long prayer time, and I thanked Him. Amazingly, while I stayed up there it was wonderful, floating on a cloud, completely losing touch with time. On the Friday I forgot and left our lovely cat out all night. It was a cold March one; that brought me down to earth with a bang. From then onwards I have experienced some hours in almost every day when I've felt almost totally well, yet for eight years I could never say I felt well day or night, it just varied in intensity and type of symptom.

Another strange thing occurred: almost immediately I developed a cold, the first in eight years, yet I was better. I know other sufferers who never catch anything when at their worst. My son's theory, and I think it extremely likely, is that our metabolism is fighting so hard to keep ME under control that it has no energy left to produce the usual mucus. So I probably had infections but the effect was to make my ME symptoms worse, with no outward sign only that inward devastating feeling that one's body is giving up. For me my temperature suddenly drops to produce this effect. For the last few years my routine has been as follows:

I rise at 7.15 a.m. generally nauseated with slight tummy pains and diarrhoea, get breakfast for my family and return to bed by 8.30 a.m. I sleep (not just rest; sleep is important to me) until midday or 2 p.m. according to how I feel. By now the nausea and diarrhoea has gone but I ache a lot and it is wonderful if a friend is around to give my whole body a very gentle rub. Not, I emphasise, a physiotherapy massage, just a gentle one, or the muscles become more bruised. It seems as if below the surface of the skin lies the cause of the aches and it is essential to keep my circulation moving. The outside of my upper arms and shoulders, legs, ribs, back and base of skull and neck are the worst spots, but by the end of my massage the pains really have gone and sometimes stay away for hours. I can then resume household chores and I stay by the phone from 3–4 p.m. (except on Fridays) to answer any other ME sufferers who may need to talk. Running an ME Group does make me feel a little useful. Every second month of the year ME sufferers meet in our home where we share together and encourage that vital gift so essential to all forms of caring, the gift of empathy. It is very necessary to help relieve sufferers isolation and to encourage them to speak freely about the illness and how much it has changed their life without fear of being misunderstood; also to exchange ideas about the treatment of symptoms and, most important, the best way to achieve peace of mind. When the mind is at peace I know the body can heal itself far far more effectively. I don't know how people can live happily without prayer, especially when unwell.

There have been several funny incidents because of ME which I find I have left unwritten: such as my graceful collapse in the butcher's shop, trying in vain to lie flat without being noticed. I rose to find I was covered from head to toe in blood soaked sawdust, looking just like a mouldy Sunday joint! Thank goodness for that extra most splendid sixth sense, the sense of humour.

I can well understand why the medical profession find ME so difficult to comprehend. How can one believe that suddenly it is almost impossible to stand or walk across a room yet five minutes ago quite possible? At one time of day there could be excruciating pain in the arms, yet later it could transfer to the knee or abdomen and the arm would be quite bearable. There are so many unanswered questions. Am I still infectious when at my worst? Why are Autumn and Spring the severest relapse times? Why is the same back left side of my head as tender now as it was eleven years ago? Why are certain parts of my arms so bruised and tender to touch with no bruising to show, and why if they are gently rubbed does the pain disappear for a short while? Why am I so much more emotional now than before the illness and why does my temperature rise every few weeks and chest pains last so long always on the left side and always when I'm still? Why is simply sitting perfectly still the recipe for the slow build up of the ill head feeling that can become torture in its intensity? Why do I sometimes experience acute giddiness that nearly knocks me off my chair? What is the reason for the nausea; diarrhoea; earache; blurred vision; aching eyes, arms, legs, neck, head and back; numerous facets of tenderness; sore throat; swollen throat sensations; forgetting a common word in mid-sentence; muscle tremors; burning or swollen joints; tearfulness; cold extremities; headaches; abdominal pains; extreme exhaustion and a horrid fungal infection of the lobe of my ears that defies all treatment? When standing for more than two minutes, I always have to lean on something or kneel on the edge of a chair (it's a good thing I'm a Methodist or I'd have been suspected of being drunk many a time)! Nowadays I use a stool stick so when I walk my 200 yards on good days and begin to feel blurred in mind and vision, I can unobtrusively slip the stool beneath me and with a car at hand I have real freedom.

I have been tested for allergies which showed some slightly positive results so I cut out the foods concerned altogether for several months, with little or no effect at all. I believe that my chelated minerals, extra zinc (of which I am apparently short) and daily vitamin B complex do help, but dabbling with tablets can be a drastic mistake and may have precipitated my last relapse.

Financially life has been difficult for Gra and but for a great friend's help our boys could not remain at their present school. I had to sell my car, which means that I am almost housebound in the weekdays but for lifts from friends. However, both boys have been great in their understanding, willingly taking on household chores that I cannot manage and they are quite proficient at rubbing my aching limbs or head. Gra does all my food shopping, bless him, besides many other jobs I would normally consider mine, without ever making me feel inadequate.

It is strange that I have only just been awarded any DHSS financial help, as I was far worse previously. Recently I was fortunate to have Dr Harold Trafford who actually cared enough to sit and listen to all the details. He spent nearly two hours with me, taking home literature about ME and willingly fought for what he believed to be right. This was a unique experience — to be believed by a physician who previously knew nothing of the disease and I am very grateful to him for his open mind.

Had I stopped here in 1984 I would have believed that I was slowly getting better, or at least had reached a steady plateau. For some unknown reason, although I have almost rigidly stuck to my timetable, 1985 was generally bad in a different way. In the spring I was sick every day, with a painful headache, for over two months, but could pretend all was OK for the odd hour or two when I had to face people. Then last autumn it hit me hard, again differently. The constant aching exhaustion all over, sudden shooting pains anywhere with no warning; painful patches as though skin had been torn away; my head was too painful for the softest pillow and yet sitting up made the room whirl and lying down made the aching intolerable. Light hurt my eyes, my ears constantly throbbed, and any sudden noise triggered uncontrollable tremors.

To be sociable was a real strain, the effort of talking and listening was immense, either I chatted inanely or sat like a zombie, fighting back tears; rarely did I feel like myself at all, but I looked well. The added strain was to learn that two close friends had developed ME symptoms and I found my temperature was up every day for six weeks. The implications that I was responsible for others' suffering became a torment; pictures of Helene haunted me. The fact that I was close to children every Sunday meant that I had to know the risks! I was told that it was unusual for a sufferer to remain infectious but my history and abnormal temperature made it likely; it would be best not to teach in junior church unless I felt really well, or could stay at least eight feet away from everyone. This bombshell is still taking its toll, although I can see life more clearly now.

I am so lucky to be able to adjust my life style with the full backing of my lovely family and friends, and cannot imagine the suffering of anyone unable to do so. The very character of this illness is that it can rob one of one's true personality, especially during a bad time and this is far worse than the aches, pains or exhaustion, because it's so impossible to describe and so damaging to one's ego and one's relationships. I have learned through experience that it is by accepting and not resisting that we can best beat this illness.

My life is full, with family and friends and my continual fight for the recognition of this illness. It really is important to prevent others from becoming chronically ill, through mishandling or misguided chivvying by those who intend to help.

Editor's Note

This devastating story relates what havoc can be caused when ME strikes at more than one member of the family. Characteristic points in the history are muscle twitching, giddiness and difficulty in standing, which is almost pathopneumonic of the illness. It also raises in an acute format the question of whether ME is infectious. While current medical opinion held that the syndrome was caused by an over-reaction of the patient's immune system to an inter-current virus infection, this did not arise, but now that doctors have come round to the idea of a more likely continuing virus infection (usually Coxsackie B), research should be concentrated on how the illness is spread, and what precautions, if any, should be taken while the patient is infectious; and incidentally, is a rise in temperature a reliable index of infectivity? The story of the French girl's untimely death would fit in with an acute Coxsackie myocarditis.

CASE HISTORY 11

J.M., Aged 14

'It was Just a Fluey Cold'

How rotten I was feeling. All this working, everyone saying how brainy I was when I wasn't that bright at all. It seemed now as though every Monday I had a bit of a temperature, a blocked up nose, sneezing and sore throat and I couldn't go to school. I was just going out of the front door to go to school when I burst into tears and went back to bed. This seemed to go on till about Wednesday, then I'd go back to school for the rest of the week. Everyone kept picking on me and teasing me, saying I was skiving off school. It made me depressed. This was around November 1981.

I enjoyed French and Latin and quite often came top, but maths and science were terrible and still are. I hated getting into trouble and sometimes felt red and guilty inside when someone else had done something wrong and when the teacher stared around at everyone. I never learnt anything in science, mostly because our science teacher was about 65 years old and about to retire. I think he was ill, because he really thought he saw pigs fly over Walton-on-the-Hill pond; he didn't know my name after teaching me for three years. Poor old Mr Collie!

Anyway I had some really good friends. Brian Haslam, a Canadian boy, Graham Simmonds and David Warren, a Vietnamese boy. Edmond Doyle lives next door to us, he went to the same school. I didn't enjoy much sport except football which I was no good at. I joined a badminton club and was good at it but didn't enjoy it that much, and as I was getting ill, I started not going. My parents must have been worried and so they started taking me to the doctor's.

First of all I went to our local GP. He just said it was catarrh but I felt really grotty and soon really started to ache quite quickly behind my knees even though through most of my life I have had aching legs. It seemed to ache just behind the knees all the time and I still don't understand why it's been there. Soon it started to get worse, I was spending more days at home during the week. One particular

121

day at school I remember I felt very ill, and in science I couldn't concentrate on what the teacher was saying, the noise in school sounded twice as loud as it was and I was tearing a piece of blotting paper into smaller and smaller pieces. Eventually after crying without making a noise I ran out to Matron's room and she took my temperature as she could see I was looking flushed. The temperature was very high, over 100°F. Matron immediately phoned my home to tell the person who looks after my sister, Anna, and me, Kirsten's her name, to come and collect me. I went home crying and to bed.

I'm Worse Being at School

Just before the Easter holidays, in '82, my hearing got much more sensitive and I really couldn't cope with the noise of the school. My reading and writing started to deteriorate. The Easter holiday wasn't a very happy one and during it my parents called in a private doctor to see what was wrong. He just said that there was nothing wrong with me and that I should stop messing about and go back to school after Easter. My parents didn't like the doctor at all, but took his advice in case I'd be better off.

But as we all found out it was for the worse. I felt worse every day and reading was going down hill very quickly. Let me give you examples of how hard things were. My ears were so sensitive that when an aeroplane passed by, when I was indoors, it bothered me. My legs ached so much that I had to keep having rests even when I just walked round the block. My ears popped and ached sometimes, and I spoke very softly. Not only that, I started feeling sick and going off my food.

The headmaster told me to start off at the beginning of the summer term to come between eight o'clock and two o'clock each day to school and no homework. But still I was worse and after about three weeks I stopped going completely. I don't remember much about the time between June that year and August except that I went to ear, nose and throat specialists, I had my eyes tested and mostly everything seemed to be fine. I had blurred vision though quite a lot. I do remember I had to have my first blood test taken and the nurse hadn't taken one properly before and she had Parkinson's disease my Mum thought. It hurt a lot.

We started going to a lady psychologist in London, all of my family, but nothing came of that. Then my parents heard of St George's Hospital where there was a child psychiatrist. We started going there and then a thing happened which was the best thing that year! In early August we were all set to go on holiday to Florida in America. I was a bit nervous about going on the aeroplane but I was surprised because the noise didn't bother me that much. We were lucky, it must have been a quiet plane. Usually when the plane takes off I have dreadful pains in my ears because of the pressure, but I am fine once I am up there.

Well, I really had a good time there for three weeks. I didn't feel unwell at all except when we went to Disneyland. You can go in one day from nine o'clock in the morning until two the next day and around midnight there are fireworks, but I felt ill around ten o'clock so we had to go back to our motel. But I enjoyed all of it apart from that time. When I came back from America in early September, everyone thought I was so much better and I thought I was as well. Then when I saw Dr Cameron at St George's Hospital to report on the holiday, he was very pleased with me and said that I should be able to try school out. I thought that I was capable of it now as well, so at the beginning of the autumn term of '82 I started, but it turned out to be awful. I felt as bad as in the last summer term and maybe worse. I felt sick and now I was having bad sleepless nights and so after about two weeks I stopped going to school completely.

Mrs Trevor

Some things I haven't told you about are that I had an infection on my fingers for which I had some cream on a prescription (I had had this for about a year) and in the summer I was put on special tablets for depression. They didn't seem to make much difference, but I can't be sure.

Around October, my Mum applied for someone to look after me between 8.30 and two o'clock when she went to work as I was staying at home to relax and recover because school was too hard for me. Eventually, I liked a lady called Mrs Trevor who lived a few roads away. So she started coming. She was quite pleasant to be with; we played board games, also I made up my own board games and I still do. My other hobbies were cooking, and pop music which I enjoyed listening to.

My doctor told me that I should increase the length of walks to build up my muscles, and so every day I went for a walk around the block with Mrs Trevor but my legs were really aching and I had to have rests on the way. All through my life I have had aches behind the knees, but not as bad as this. I put my fingers in my ears when cars went by as the noise didn't seem so loud then. I still couldn't read or write but Dr Cameron said I was getting better when we went to see him every six weeks. One thing that I haven't pointed out is that concentration was mainly the reason for all these problems. I could see the writing in books, for instance, most of the time but I couldn't concentrate on putting the letters together. That was the same as the writing and I couldn't get myself to run around or even ride a bicycle.

In February, a week after my birthday in '83, Dr Cameron said I had to go to Atkinson Morely Hospital for a brain scan and maybe a few other things, perhaps staying in a few days. I didn't really want to go there, because I hated being without my parents especially overnight. But the morning I went, I made friends with a boy. In the late afternoon I went to the scanning room and had my brain looked at. The doctors told me that I could go home the same night because they found that brain tissue was scarred and I had a virus. Well, nothing much happened for the next month, except that we were told that I had the symptoms of the virus myalgic encephalomyelitis and frequently my mum went to their club.

Around this time, I seemed to feel quite happy inside myself and right at the beginning of April my parents, my sister and my grandparents went on holiday to Guernsey for a week with me. Dr Cameron told me that I needed the break. Anyway, I quite enjoyed myself there except for one time which I remember. One of the days we were there I was mucking about with my sister on the stairs and I did somersaults down the stairs and for the day afterwards I felt unwell and dizzy but it was partly my fault.

A Step in the Wrong Direction

Around this time, maybe it was before April, my bath one night was hot and when I got out I felt dizzy. I was even hallucinating, but I think the next morning I felt alright. At the beginning of May my Mum had to go to Torquay for a conference or something like that for a week and as my grandparents live in Devon Dr Cameron told my parents that I needed a break in the countryside, therefore my

Mum should drop me off at Honiton and then go on to Torquay for the week and collect me the next Saturday. I wasn't looking forward to going down because I hadn't stayed somewhere for a whole week without my family since my illness had started. But on the Monday we went down in the car and arrived in the early evening.

On Tuesday afternoon my Mum said goodbye to me. I burst out crying and couldn't bear to see her leaving. To think I had to put up without her for a week. When she left I felt awful and started to feel sick with tension. The next day I felt worse and thought at that moment that it was the worst time of my life. I stayed in bed for most of the week because as I was feeling so sick all I remember eating was cereal and mint choc chip ice-cream. I was very unhappy and phoned up Mum every night. She seemed quite worried about me, not surprisingly, but I didn't want to let my Dad and sister know how bad I was, as I didn't want them to worry. The only time that I was happy was when I watched a comedy film and I laughed a bit.

Mum picked me up on the Saturday, and I felt much closer to her. She thanked my Nan for looking after me so well and when we got back my Dad seemed shocked by how bad I was as he didn't know that I was so ill. My legs ached a lot and therefore I couldn't walk much at all. I still wasn't eating much either and even though over the next couple of weeks I had ups, I had more downs so in the beginning of June I was admitted to Great Ormond Street Hospital in London for tests.

I must have been there for about two weeks and even though I don't remember much about it I know that the loud noises got on top of me (drilling, children being noisy and so on) so much that I slowly got worse. I ached less and talked less each day but I remember thinking up a poem about a man in hospital which was quite amazing because I wasn't talking or concentrating much. My Dad spent half a day with me in my room and then he went back to work when my Mum stayed with me.

The Poem I Dictated to my Mum in Great Ormond Street Hospital (17.6.83)

> There was a man who was very poorly,
> So he was taken to Atkinson Morely.
> He was taken to hospital by ambulance,
> And on the way he wet his pants,

He was taken there for he had an infection,
And so they gave him an injection,
Next he was given a blood test,
And it didn't give him any rest,
He was treated by the nurse,
Which made him even worse.
He didn't really like the sister,
Because she gave him an awful blister
By standing on his weak toes,
And then she had to change his clothes.
She tickled his feet, to make him eat,
But it was a trick and made him sick.
The doctor tested him with his stethoscope,
But he never ever spoke.
The patient couldn't stand the noise,
Because of the boys playing with their toys,
Then at last he had an EEG,
But he didn't know what the result would be,
They forced him to have a blanket bath,
But this meant they needed all the staff,
Then they gave him a brain scan,
Which started to make him a well man,
But he still had nightmares in the night,
And really needed to keep on the light.
Then the doctor gave him an encouraging letter,
And this began to make him feel better,
He really had been in such pain,
He never wanted to be in hospital again,
This is the end of his hospital tale,
For it was almost like being in jail!

After lots of blood tests and other things I left Great Ormond
Street because after about two weeks of being there I stopped
walking and talking completely and as they saw I was getting worse
they discharged me. Well after that, I never wanted to go in hospital
again. I stayed up in my bedroom all the time and didn't do anything
except cry. For a week my parents stayed with me most of the time
but in early July, until the summer holidays began, Mrs Trevor
started looking after me in the mornings. It was terrible. She kept on
bending over me when I was in my bed and giving me food and
poking it in front of me, in a strict voice telling me to eat it. I don't

know if you can imagine it but she really seemed like a monster to me. And when she wasn't there, I imagined her speaking to me and her face on the walls. My Mum realised that she was making me so much worse that she sacked her. But that made me feel no better.

Slowly Improving

By the way, a few years before my illness started, I had a dream quite frequently about dinosaurs trying to get into our house through my bedroom window and now I kept on imagining it throughout the day, also seeing monsters on my wall.

My Dad had broken up from the school that he was teaching at and didn't spend a very happy holiday. He brought me up a special drink called 'Clinifeed' which I had to drink four times a day. I found it very difficult to drink it because it was so sickly and I was feeling very sick. I found it hard to concentrate on anything and I only sometimes understood what people were saying. This happened for quite a long time afterwards. I couldn't concentrate on speaking at all, but I had watched the television programme 'Give Us A Clue' quite a lot before so I mimed what I wanted to say a lot of the time and made whines. The radio was on for most of the day and all the pop tunes from that time which I hear now make me feel horrible inside and I don't like any of them. I hardly smiled at all and I was beginning to give up hope, thinking that I'd never get better, also that I would eventually die. I did want to eat but I felt so sick, I couldn't.

I was put on more tablets. I had a sleeping tablet every night now because I didn't get to sleep until at least eleven o'clock each night, for feeling sick and worrying about seeing monsters in my dream. Therefore, I had my light on all night long. Also I had bad bowel trouble. I found it very difficult to go to the toilet even when on tablets, probably because I was not moving about.

One day some nurses came from St George's Hospital to see me and so the night before my Dad put me in the bath to be clean but I kicked and screamed. I hated water from then on. I remembered the time when I was three years old and we were on holiday. I nearly drowned in the sea and for a couple of years afterwards I could see myself under the water, and so from then on my Mum used some special watered tissues to wipe me all over.

As I couldn't concentrate on anything like reading or television the days passed very slowly, even though I can't remember much about this period except one thing, and maybe the only thing which I enjoyed doing, was playing with 'Fuzzy Felts'. It kept me occupied, constructing pictures.

At about the beginning of October '83, things seemed to start changing. I felt more hopeful that I was going to get better and more positive. For instance, I felt less sick each day, and I think one day when my Dad brought me up some 'Clinifeed', I signalled to him that I wanted to try ordinary food. So, he brought some up and I ate a small amount. This was to lead me, over the next month or two into eating perfectly normally.

Also around this time a man called Trevor, who maybe was a faith healer, came round to our house once a week to pray for me. One day, I asked my Mum to help me out of bed, (by signalling) and I tried to stand up. This was a tremendous effort for me but I was pleased with myself and felt more confident to walk. So over the next few days, I started to move a few paces with great concentration needed when my parents came back from work. About two weeks after I had stood up, I found myself being able to walk outside in the garden being supported by my Mum or Dad but I still found the birds' singing distracting me from concentrating on walking.

Even though I was eating normally and walking better I still had bowel problems, sleeping problems, seeing monsters and Mrs Trevor, not speaking, aching legs and not understanding what people said sometimes, because of bad concentration. Maybe it seems to you that Trevor might have helped me but I don't think he did. I really thought that 1984 was going to be a great year and was going to be the year that I would get completely better and go back to school. But I was wrong.

That Lawn Mower

Christmas '83 wasn't too bad. I thought that I might have been walking unassisted but I couldn't. My legs felt weaker and at the end of December I stopped walking and just crawled around on my knees.

The lady who looked after me from October until this time was Mrs Powell who lives just over the road. I really enjoyed her company but she didn't want to look after me anymore so my Mum phoned up places to see if she could find someone who would want to look after me. A few people came over to our house but the only one I liked was a lady called Maureen. So, my Mum agreed that she would come for three days a week. The other two days my Mum stayed home in the morning and Kirsten stayed in the afternoon.

At the beginning of January, I made up a board game. It took a lot of concentration but I enjoyed it though I found it hard to explain the rules as I wasn't talking. This was a good achievement but when Maureen started coming I felt rather uneasy and a little sick. Bad news came when Mum only stayed home for one day during the week and that made me very depressed. I couldn't help what happened next. I ate less and less once more and I stayed in bed all the time as I couldn't get up and about at all. Not only that, being in bed all the time made me so depressed that I must have been crying for three hours a day. This must have made Maureen unhappy but I couldn't help it. By the way, I didn't really feel depressed much at the weekends when the family was home. I had definitely relapsed again.

At this time I was only eating mince and yoghurt and I was losing weight. February seemed exactly the same as January. I can't really remember my birthday or much of February at all. But in early March a new face appeared on the scene. My Dad had seen an article in the newspaper about some people who had helped children who had been ill by feeling and rubbing the parts of the body that were wrong. They were experienced osteopaths and my Dad thought that they would help me. So one Sunday, Johnathan and Kathryn Curtis-Lake came to our house. They had a chat with my parents, saw me and decided that Kathryn should start treating me.

She came once a week, I think, and I lay down upside down on the bed and she felt my head and rubbed my legs, and so on. She could tell, just by feeling my head, that I still had scarred tissue in my brain, and the messages weren't getting through to the legs. I felt sleepy after she had finished with me but felt better in the long run. At this time for about one week, without my parents or anyone knowing, I tried to stand up on my own, hoping that I could get to eventually walk on my own and surprise my parents that I could. I was determined and I managed to stand up but got nowhere else because of something that happened roughly the next week.

At the end of March, one day during the week in the afternoon the gardener next door started up his lawn mower and the noise was too much for me even though I had double glazing in my bedroom window. I was screaming out and crying as it sounded so loud and then what I realised was that my sister was coming home late from school and I was upset because I get on very well with her and to top it all Trevor came that afternoon dressed in a robe and a wooden cross around his neck. That scared me so much, I really thought that he was taking me up to heaven. I was going to die! I screamed for ages. I don't remember what happened afterwards but I had gone back again. The result was that I was more sensitive to noise and my vision became quite blurred most of the time but the most different thing was that I couldn't bear to be without my parents or my sister for one minute of the day. It seemed that I was never going to get better.

Fortunately, it was the start of the school holidays and so my sister and Dad could look after me, staying in my bedroom most of the day. I remember that one day I didn't even like the sound of Dad turning over a page of the newspaper that he was reading. Poor Mum and Dad. All the worry they had over me that last year. They must have had a lot of patience. I was so mixed up inside me, I couldn't concentrate on any activity except one thing that I enjoyed doing. I had some cardboard buildings bought for me and when they were all put together I used to push cars around them as if in a village.

Conking Out

I don't remember it but once, a few weeks ago, my sister told me that at around this time I threw a board at her and it hurt her. I can't recall why I did it though. Certainly I felt bad, but with Kathryn treating me I started feeling a bit better physically. At the end of April, the crucial time came. My Dad couldn't take any more days off and the summer term was starting, so he had to go back to work. The trouble was that I couldn't bear to be without Mum and Dad as they had been with me for a month all the time. So one day, at the beginning of May, after they must have thought that I would be alright and wouldn't get worse they went to work, probably leaving Maureen in the house. Even though it was about four hours, I screamed all the time and for about 30 minutes (though I am not sure) I went sort of unconscious. Then waking up, screaming, and going unconscious again.

My Mum told me recently that at one time I stopped breathing for quite a long time and had to be resuscitated by Kathryn. I did this kind of thing for about two weeks and then, after that, I did what I call 'conking out' for virtually all the day until my parents came home from work and they patted my face or lifted up my eyelids to wake me up. Then they would stay with me most of the evening and all I could do was try my best to move my cars around and listen to the pop charts. I tried my best to watch 'Top of the Pops' on the black and white television but on most occasions, (but not always) my vision was too blurred to see the picture. Then at nights I slept with my Mum. I had done this since Easter and since then my nightmares had become rare and I was sleeping quite well.

Since Easter, my Nan and Grandpa had been here, looking after me and the house. They were very concerned. One Sunday around May time, my Nan and Grandpa went to church and Grandpa passed out. He was taken to hospital and with me to cope with as well it was a trying day for everyone, I am sure. As I was getting worse I felt so depressed. I felt I would never get better and I really wanted to die. What was there to live for anyway?

One thing I haven't told you is that I would only accept my sister and parents in the room (not being horrible, but that I was really frightened of other people) and if anyone else came into the room, I would scream for about five seconds and then conk out until someone woke me up. Sometimes, (depending on how deep a sleep I went into) when I conked out I knew what was going on around me, but not always. Also my sensitivity to noise was worse and any little sound made me conk out. Other problems were still there, of course speaking, walking and bowel trouble, headaches and eating. I was only eating about three yoghurts a day, and only when they were passed to me. Also one other problem; being on my own all day long, I started urinating in the bed. It was terrible, but what could I do?

On to the beginning of June '84, now, and a completely new aspect to my illness. This is very hard to explain, but I would say that about once every three days I managed to get up and actually walk — just a few paces, but it was amazing! The mental block just went away for a few minutes, but never when someone was in the room. I wanted to show Mum and Dad that I could walk but I just couldn't do it. This got me worked up but I could still walk a bit. I think the same kind of pattern carried on for two months. I also was very frightened of our cat which seemed like an enormous tiger to me. This illness might have carried on for years if it wasn't for a decision that was to change my life!

Colwood

It was strange, because in the middle of July, I started to improve but that didn't make any difference because yet again I relapsed, just a little because before I knew it, I was whisked away — must have been when I conked out for a whole day — to a hospital 40 miles away in Haywards Heath called Colwood. It is an adolescent unit for children with problems such as school refusers, bad behaviour and not getting on well with their family.

I find it very hard to remember what happened the first few weeks I was there. It was the first time since Devon that I had been away from home and I was very distressed even though I couldn't show it. I was so homesick, I used to see an illusion of my Mum on the wall and whined out to her. But most of August, I was conked out 75 per cent of the time. I can't really remember much about it, but I went to another hospital for a week, right at the beginning of August (just a week after I had come into Colwood) because I hadn't eaten anything but it didn't do any good so I came back to Colwood.

When I hadn't conked out, I just lay down thinking, feeling awful, not even moving my hands except I had moments when I could move my hands and occasionally get up and walk about. I didn't want anyone to know that I could move otherwise they would think I could do it all the time if I wanted when I couldn't. I've been told lately that one day Sue, one of the nurses, saw me walking all the way over to the bathroom, take a drink and go back. She probably went back and told all the other nurses and of course they didn't understand that I *couldn't* move when they were around and not *wouldn't*.

Sometimes when my vision wasn't blurred and I wasn't conked out, I saw that the nurses could see me move but I didn't care. I tried to move but I suddenly went like a zombie again when they saw me; my mental block just came back again. Occasionally, even though I felt so sick and knew that I would swallow air like a baby when I ate, I ate a bit of anything if I had one of my good moments because I knew I would die if I didn't. I really didn't want to die at this time even though I thought I would be stuck in this room for years to come.

Some things I've been told lately but don't remember, are that one week in August the nurses took me in a wheelchair to Brighton beach but I didn't do anything, I always just stayed lying on the ground eyes closed, dead to the world almost. Also I was taken to the cinema and one day I was sitting outside and a wasp went right around my mouth and stung me, but still I didn't move. The nurses bathed me most days (I just remember this) and as I was scared of water as soon as they plopped me into the bath I conked out. I still was wetting myself and I conked out and found it awful just lying there when I couldn't tell anyone that I had wetted myself. All of this time I had always wanted to be able to walk around, talk and so on but I just couldn't. I don't really think I made much effort then to get better.

At the beginning of September I was put on a drip-feed system with a tube down my nose. Amazingly I didn't find that it hurt at all and actually thought it was marvellous that I was having nourishment without feeling sick or burping. This went on for about three weeks; me just lying in my bed, not doing anything and even when having one of my good moments not able to move because I was tied to the drip-feed system.

Around this time, I really can't remember what I ever thought about (occasionally thinking about pop music but otherwise a total blank) that month seems now like just a couple of days! As you can see on the chart, nothing was any better in September, my sensitivity to noise was the same level, I still felt very depressed, but in October things started to change!

Progression

My parents had come twice since I had come to Colwood in July. I don't remember seeing them at all on the first occasion but on the second which was in October, I managed the first smile for over half a year. (From the last February onwards I always went into a tantrum when I had just smiled, I still don't really know why.)

At the end of September the nurses decided to take me off tube-feeding because that wasn't encouraging me to make the effort of eating myself and so they switched to feeding me with normal food and using a syringe after mashing it up to squirt down into my throat. It was a very painful experience (as I had trouble swallowing anyway and I took down even more air this way) but I knew that I couldn't do anything about it. I felt more sick than ever and felt so awful that I thought that I'd never eat properly again. I hardly ever felt angry with the nurses because they didn't understand how I felt and so just did what they thought was right. (I'm not the sort of person who loses his temper anyway) but a couple of the male nurses treated me roughly by slapping my face, shouting at me and hurling me around the room. I suppose they wanted me to snap out of my own little world but they went a bit too far.

At the beginning of October I was no longer in my bedroom all day but around the place in the lounge, the dining room, even over at the little school which was connected with the hospital by being pushed along everywhere in a wheelchair. It was a change of plan so that I was being with all the other kids and it might stimulate me and they could try and help me which they did — a lot! Most of the kids sat with me and encouraged me to move my arm or something like that. Nothing happened for about a week and then, with their encouragement (which I needed) I made an enormous effort, and I lifted my arm in the air! It was the first time I had done that with people present since July. I was very pleased with myself and over the next couple of weeks I tried a little harder and managed to lift up both arms and wave them around. One boy called Wayne stayed with me for ages, encouraging me to move my arms about. And a girl called Adele stayed with me a lot as well.

Nearing the end of October, one morning I woke up (by the way I conked out each night when the light was turned off and gradually fell asleep and was then woken up by the staff) and didn't feel sick any more! I waited until breakfast and when Caroline (one of the nurses) gave me my Weetabix and then went off to fetch a syringe to use I picked up the spoon and started eating it. It actually tasted quite nice! When Caroline came back she must have been surprised. I was certainly pleased. Well I think I don't have to mention food again in this book because from then on I have eaten perfectly normally.

For the next few weeks I was very happy, still not talking, walking, going to the toilet properly or bearing much noise although it was getting better, but my vision seemed virtually normal now. I was now helping the nurse to get me dressed and I started tapping or clapping my hands to the beats of pop songs which took a lot of concentration but was the first bit of co-ordination for a long time. And all the kids helped me a lot from then onwards. I think that the kids actually helped me to get better more than anything else. From then on I thought that life was for living after all!

A Little Swimming Lesson

I wasn't homesick anymore, I was used to Colwood now. I was still not reading or writing and I conked out whenever the kids ran around screaming or if there was any noise. Now that I was improving, the nurses took me outside in my wheelchair but as soon as I went out of the front door I just conked out because I had been stuck inside for so long, I had become a kind of agoraphobic so it wasn't much good taking me out except for the fresh air! It was then decided that I needed exercising so as there were swimming periods each day during the week, I would be wheeled down there and go in the pool while somebody would move my legs up and down.

It happened and it was terrible. No-one seemed to realise that I had a fear of water and putting me in that pool made my fear a whole lot worse. I stayed awake in the changing room while I was being changed but as soon as I touched the water I conked out. My eyes were opened by whoever was holding me up time and time again but it was no good. I started shivering. I felt so dizzy, so terrible; might all of this recovery of the last month go away and I become seriously ill again? In the pool I actually wanted to conk out to get away from everything, whereas normally when I conked out I tried not to but I couldn't help it. When I was taken out of the pool I couldn't make any effort to help get changed back. I felt so weak and distressed. My head was spinning around and I still conked out every four minutes or so.

I was still distressed for about 25 minutes after coming out of the pool each day. I went down to the swimming pool for about three weeks and then one day just as I was about to be taken down, I threw my trunks and towel off the side of the wheelchair and on to the floor. I really hated going and I thought that maybe I could practice trying to walk instead of going swimming. So I used my two fingers to make the sign of walking to the nurses. They understood what I meant and so, instead of going swimming that day the nurses held me up, one either side and I supported myself for the first time since August when I had done it on my own. And then building up all my concentration, and trying to forget that anyone was there, I managed to move one small pace on my own and then collapsed and conked out. But I felt very proud of myself.

This was all happening around the middle of November and things were progressing all the time. I was still occasionally taken down to the swimming pool but mostly I practised trying to walk.

Then over at the school Dave, my teacher, set up a kind of programme for me to try and start speaking. I found it very difficult to make any noise at all but the kids in my class encouraged me and I managed to make a humming sound. As the days went by, I managed to say a couple of words after taking about 30 seconds of concentration, the words being 'Mummy' and 'Anna' possibly. Then I managed over the next couple of weeks to build my vocabulary up to ten words with an effort. It gave me a headache each time but was worth it. Dave had been making a video of me all of this time showing my progress.

At the beginning of December, my swimming had been stopped completely and I started to draw (which was an amazing achievement). It also took an awful lot of concentration and it ended up to be a very long picture. In the first week of December, my mother and father came to see me again and were so delighted to see me, and vice versa. It was the first time that they heard me say a couple of words for 18 months. Then we all went in to the room of my consultant, Dr Etkin, and he surprised us all when he asked me if I would like to go home for a few hours in two days time! I managed to say yes and we were all so pleased. It was going to be the first time that I had been home for five months!

I now fully understood what people were saying whereas before I didn't all the time, and the nurses said that I should make a really big effort to walk before I went home which I did, but not enough because I went home on that Sunday with a wheelchair to be pushed around in by my Mum or Dad or sister.

Christmas Cheer

I thoroughly enjoyed myself for the six hours that I was home and a couple of the neighbours came around to see me and I managed to say hello and goodbye to them. As the afternoon at home went so well, it was planned that I should I go home and spend a night the next weekend and from then onwards, spend the whole weekend at home, which is what happened.

The first Wednesday after I went home for the day, I woke up in the morning and felt that my head was so much clearer. I could concentrate on particular things and especially speaking. I could now speak perfectly normally and when one of the nurses came to get me out of bed I easily said 'good morning' to him and he was surprised. All day I went around saying 'hello' and making conversation to everyone and I felt so happy and pleased with myself. I told Dr Etkin that I wanted to surprise my Dad and talk to him and so he phoned up my Dad at work and he was shocked to hear all of these sentences come spurting out of my mouth and went home and told my family. Surprisingly enough, exactly a week after I started talking, my effort of walking step by step was rewarded when I straight away, when I woke up, managed to walk normally!

My head felt so much clearer yet again and now I was able to do so many more things. I could get dressed on my own and walk around in the unit without a wheelchair. I had once felt very close to Adele since she had helped me a lot in the months before but she didn't seem all that close to me now. I could now think about talking to all the other kids and try to help them.

Just before Colwood broke up for the Christmas holidays Dave arranged a kind of play for the kids to act out, to perform in front of the staff and some parents at the Christmas party. And would you believe that I was the main actor in it! Yes, I was, and Dave was taking a big risk in making me the main character as I had only been walking for a week and I was just standing up for over half an hour solidly. My legs still ached an enormous amount when I was walking for a while.

The play went very well and everyone loved it including me. Then it was off home for a two-week long Christmas holiday which I enjoyed tremendously. I hardly went outside at all because I still had a fear of going out (mainly because of the cars looking like monsters a bit) but I still received lots of presents, and every day different friends and relations came round to see how I was. They were so pleased and I was proud of myself.

Would you like a run-down of all my problems from then? Well, I still had slight bowel trouble; my sensitivity to noises was still bad but gradually getting better; my legs still ached; I had a fear of going out; I found it frightening to have a bath (I felt dizzy and faint); I couldn't read or write at all and I couldn't express feelings of anger.

I enjoyed Christmas an awful lot, and came to Colwood at the beginning of January to start a new year, 1985. During the end of my Christmas holiday, I started to gradually go further outside each day, holding on to my Mum or Dad on the way (only because I needed support if I conked out, which I was still doing outside on occasions). It took a lot of effort to keep calm and stay awake outside because I obviously wanted not to conk out and get better.

Hyperventilating I think, was the only cause of why I conked out.

So, soon after I came back to Colwood, with the nurses' (and some of the kids') help, I gradually felt easier about being outside, and in the middle of January, on the last day that I found going outdoors difficult it was also the last day that I have ever conked out.

Schoolwork

Adele was anorexic and she had been at Colwood for three months and now she was better; so she left one Friday. I really was very upset because I cared for her so much and I felt depressed at times for the following two weeks. I don't find it easy to talk to anyone when I am upset and at that time I could only talk to Dyanne, one of the nurses. Anyway Adele came back for a check-up each week for a while and I looked forward to that.

At the end of January I had not many problems left. My sensitivity to noise was completely normal (this was proved because I was now going to the local disco the Albermarle each Thursday, and that was pretty noisy); I was going to the toilet alright; talking normally, my walking was fine except that when I walked down the road my legs started aching; I still had a fear of water surrounding me which was getting better though, and I couldn't read or write at all which was difficult to live with, but it wasn't very long before that was changed. At the beginning of February, Dave started trying to teach me to learn to read again. He went through the letters of the alphabet first and then asked me to read difficult letters. He was very helpful and after three difficult weeks I managed to read and write perfectly normally. Another problem out of the way!

I still dreaded having a bath twice a week. I felt fine when I was changing but once I put my foot in the water, I started to panic and once I had sat in the bath I hyperventilated and remembered the time when I nearly drowned being underneath the water. It took a lot of effort not to conk out and I never did from then onwards.

I had a good birthday, the kids gave me presents, Melissa gave me a mug, David gave me some hair gel and I got a poster from Jason. By the way, I was friends with everyone at Colwood now and I liked it there because I felt I had grown up again. As a birthday treat in March the family went to see the musical 'Starlight Express' which was very loud; too loud for my Mum and Dad, but fine for me. I really enjoyed it.

In March I started going home on Fridays on the train alone. At first I found it difficult but after a couple of weeks I found it easy. I started to feel more independent. I also now started going back to the swimming pool (of my own free will) once a week and gradually going from dipping my feet in to standing up in the shallow end and walking along. I found it very difficult as I had bad memories of the trips down there five months ago.

Over the next month or so I progressed slowly. Trying to help the other kids with their problems, slowly finding it easier to have a bath, helping around the house and in the garden over the two-week Easter holiday and working a lot harder with Dave in school — I actually did an English 'O' level exam paper, some French exercises, maths and writing stories. I still occasionally couldn't concentrate on working though, my mind just went blank. I enjoyed playing badminton and making up games. Even though I'm not that good, I enjoy cooking as well. I got depressed about once every week, thinking that I wasn't any good at anything and I hated myself. Quite often it happened when I was playing a team game and I felt that I was letting the team down.

In the middle of April I faced a new adventure. I started going to tennis lessons at home every weekend which was the first time that I had to do a coached sport and meet a lot of new people since I was first ill, but as the weeks went on I enjoyed it more and now I love playing tennis and I've made a friend there, Paul.

Warden Park

To think that only six months ago, I was motionless, speechless and not eating! Only one more fear to face up to — school; and that was all to happen over the next two months. At the beginning of May, Dave told me that I was going to have a look round a school, just three miles away from Colwood. I was very nervous, as I hadn't been to a proper school for three years and I went with Barry (the headmaster at Colwood) to the school called Warden Park. I had an interview for half an hour with Mr Smith, the deputy headmaster and looked around. It was enormous.

Soon it was agreed that I was to start at Warden Park about a week later. So on the Monday for just three hours that week, I was driven there. I was scared stiff about meeting all of the kids and teachers. I was so frightened about school because of the bad memories I had of being at school when I was ill. At the first lesson I didn't talk but got on with the home economics. In the second lesson (English) I felt so depressed because I thought that the teacher was going to ask me to read in front of the class. He never did! For weeks afterwards (and I'm still going) I went to Warden Park, stepping up the times each week. From half a day to two, three and four half days and at the moment I'm going there for two whole days and two half days. I still sometimes get depressed after school and I use up so much energy at school that I have none left afterwards. The first week I went to Warden Park for a full day I felt so bad that I locked myself in the toilet for 20 minutes. I felt so lonely. Also in the middle of June I started going there by bus on my own. At first I was really frightened about going but it turned out alright. Also I still feel awful and tense when I play games or PE, I feel that I'm letting the team down and that I'm no good. But over the past month, I have made five friends at Warden Park and I'm beginning to feel more normal.

A couple of weeks ago I went to a school in Sutton (where I live) for an exam and interview. I'm going to Warden Park until July and then I may be going to this other school in September. School is still difficult for me but I'm overcoming all the hurdles. I still find it difficult to talk to people when I'm depressed and I cannot get angry with other people. I think that because I don't get angry with anyone else I let it out on myself and that's why I get depressed. When I get in the bath I feel just a little dizzy and hot but I don't get frightened. I'm going to California in August and I'll be in the water then. I hope I will be alright. I will enjoy it though.

I think that I became ill partly because of the virus and partly because too much pressure was put on me previously at school to work hard. Also I set myself high standards and not getting angry could have played a part as well.But I'm sure that I won't be ill again. Colwood has done a lot for me. Not only helped me get better but build up my confidence a lot. I will leave shortly and will have to face reality. A lot of effort will be needed on my part and it will be difficult for me to cope. But I'll manage. I think. I know.

Editor's Note

This is a courageous story which the author must have struggled to relate and deserves credit for telling. It is encouraging that after such a traumatic illness he is now slowly beginning to get better. It is more the story of a particularly virulent viral encephalomyelitis rather than a post-viral syndrome, but the excessive sensitivity to noise, depression, sleeping problems and difficulty in concentrating are typical of ME. Other patients have also complained of faintness and giddiness when having a bath and feeling as though they were going to die.

USEFUL ADDRESSES

United Kingdom

Mrs Pam Searles
Hon. Secretary
UK ME Association
PO Box 8
Stanford le Hope
Essex SS17 8EX
(0375) 642466

United States of America

C.F.I.D.S. Association
Community Health Services
PO Box 220398
Charlotte
North Carolina
USA 28222–0398

National C.F.I.D.S. Society
PO Box 230108
8905 S.W. Commercial Street
Suite B
Portland
Oregon
USA 97223

National CFS Association
919 Scott Avenue
Kansas City
Kansas
USA 66105

North West C.F.I.D.S. Voice
c/o N.W. C.F.I.D.S. Voice

6335 51st Avenue South
Seattle
Washington
USA 98118

CFIDS Support Group
c/o Jewish Community Center of Greater Rochester
1200 Edgewood Avenue
PO Box 18997
Rochester
New York
USA 14618–0997

Australia

ME/Chronic Fatigue Syndrome Society Inc.
PO Box 7
Moonee Ponds
Victoria 3039
Australia

ME Soc. New South Wales
ANZMES NSW
PO Box 645
Mona Vale 2103
New South Wales
Australia

Allergy Association Australia
Ms M. Bowes, Pres.
PO Box 45
Woody Point
Queensland 4019
Australia

ME Society Inc. (S.A. Support Group)
Lyn Drysdale
PO Box 383
Adelaide
South Australia 5001
Australia

New Zealand

ANZMES
Jim Brook Church
PO Box 35–429
Browns Bay
Auckland 10
New Zealand

South Africa

Mrs Janine Shavell
ME Awareness Group
66 Third Street
Lower Houghton
Johannesburg
South Africa

Canada

ME Association of Canada
400–426 Queen Street
Ottawa
Ontario
Canada K1P 5E4

The Nightingale Research Foundation
36 Kenora Street
Ottawa
Ontario
Canada K1Y 3K8

Ireland

Miriam and Peter Sheridan
80 Foxfield Road
Raehny
Dublin 5
Eire

Norway

Norges ME Forening
Ellen Piro
Gullerasveien 14B
0386
Oslo 3
Norway

Netherlands

ME Stichting
Patients Information
PO Box 116
1120 A.C. Landsmeer
Netherlands

BIBLIOGRAPHY OF LITERATURE ON MYALGIC ENCEPHALOMYELITIS

This bibliography is listed in alphabetical order, with recommended papers starred. The reader's attention is drawn to the *Nursing Times*, 27 April 1978, which is probably the best source for lay readers; the *Post Graduate Medical Journal*, November 1978, which is the most comprehensive work for health professionals; and to the article by Behan *et al.* (1985) for the most up-to-date medical paper on patients they have examined.

Literature up to 1980

Acheson, E.D. (1954) *Lancet, ii,* 1944
—— (1955) ibid., *ii,* 394
*—— (1959) *American Journal of Medicine, 26,* 569
Albrecht, R.M. *et al.* (1964) *Journal of the American Medical Association, 187,* 904
Brain, Lord, and Walton, J.N. (1969) 'Benign Myalgic Encephalomyelitis' in *Diseases of the Nervous System,* 7th edn, Oxford University Press, London, New York and Toronto
British Medical Journal (1978) Lead Article. *1,* 1436
*Compston, N. *et al.* (1970) *British Medical Journal, 1,* 362
Corridan, J.P. (1976) *Journal of the Irish Medical Association, 69,* 414
Cotterill, J. (1973) *Lancet, i,* 1308
Crowley, N. *et al.* (1957) *Journal of Hygiene, (Cambridge), 55,* 102
Deisher, J.B. (1957) *Northwest Medicine, 56,* 1451
Dillon, M.J. *et al.* (1974) *British Medical Journal, i,* 301
Gilliam, A.G. (1938) *Public Health Bulletin,* No. 240
Graybill, J.A. *et al.* (1972) *Journal of the American Medical Association, 219,* 1440
Hart, R.H. (1969) *New England Journal of Medicine, 281,* 797
Henderson, D.A. and Shelokov, A. (1959) *New England Journal of Medicine, 260,* 757
Hicks, D.A. (1957) *Lancet, i,* 686
Hill, R.C.J. *et al.* (1959) ibid. *i,* 689
Houghton, L.E. and Jones E.I. (1942) ibid., *i,* 196
Igata, A. (1971) ibid., *ii,* 43
Innes S.G.B. (1970) ibid., *i,* 969
Innoue,Y.K. *et al.* (1971) ibid., *i,* 853
—— *et al.* (1972) ibid., *ii,* 705
Jackson, A.L. *et al.* (1957) *South African Medical Journal, 31,* 514
Jackson, J.R. (1952) 14th Annual Report South Australian Institute of Medical and Veterinary Science, July 1951–July 1952, p.17
Jelinek, J.E. (1956) *Lancet, ii,* 494
Kendall, R.E. (1967) *British Journal of Psychiatry, 113,* 833
Lowe, C.K. and Lwanga, S.K. (1978) *Health Statistics,* p.44. Oxford Medical publication

Lyle, W.H. (1959) 'An outbreak of disease believed to have been caused by Echo 9 virus.' *Annals of Internal Medicine, 51;2,* 248

Macrae, A.D. and Galpine, J.F. (1954) *Lancet, ii,* 350

*Medical Staff of the Royal Free Hospital (1957) *British Medical Journal, ii; 19,* 50

Nakae, K. *et al.* (1971) *Lancet, ii,* 41

Nursing Times (1978) April 27th. This issue includes four articles on ME

Parish J.G. (1970) *British Medical Journal, i,* 47

—— (1974) Medical Science Editorial, *Journal of International Research Communications, 2,* 22

Pederson, E.P. (1956) *Danish Medical Bulletin, 3,* 65

Pellew, R.A. (1951) *Medical Journal of Australia, 1,* 944

—— and Miles, J.A.E. (1955) ibid., *42,* 480

Pool, J.H. *et al.* (1961) *Lancet, i,* 733

Postgraduate Medical Journal (1978) Whole of the November issue

Price, J. (1961) *Lancet, i,* 737

Ramsay, A.M. (1965) *British Medical Journal, 2,* 1062

—— (1976) *Update, 13,* 539

—— (1978) *Postgraduate Medical Journal, 54,* 1978

—— and O'Sullivan, E. (1956) *Lancet,* 761

—— and Rundle, A. (1979) ibid., *55,* 856–857

Richardson A.E. (1956) *Annals of Physical Medicine, 3,*81

Shelakov, A. (1978) in P.D. Hoprich (ed.) *Infectious Diseases.* Harper and Row, Maryland USA, p.1299

—— *et al.* (1957) *New England Journal of Medicine, 257,* 345

Sigurdsson, B. *et al.* (1950) *American Journal of Hygiene, 52,*222

—— *et al.*(1958) *Lancet, i,* 370

Sigurdsson, B. and Gudmoundsson, K.R. (1956) ibid., *i,* 766

Steen, A.S. (1956) *British Medical Journal, 1,* 235

Wallis, A.L. (1955) *Lancet, ii,* 1091

—— (1957) 'An investigation into an unusual disease seen in epidemic and sporadic form in general practice in Cumberland in 1955 and subsequent years.' MSc. Thesis, University of Edinburgh

White, D.M. and Burtch, R.B. (1954) *Neurology, 4,* 506

Literature since 1980

1980

*Behan, P. O. 'Epidemic Myalgic Encephalomyelitis.' *The Practitioner, 224,* 805

*—— and Behan, W. M. 'Epidemic Myalgic Encephalomyelitis.' in F. Clifford Rose (ed.) *Clinical Neuroepidemiology.* Pitman Medical, London

*Bishop, J. 'Epidemic Myalgic Encephalomyelitis.' *The Medical Journal of Australia, 1,* 585

*Church, A. J. 'Myalgic Encephalomyalitis — An Obscene Cosmic Joke?' (An interesting account from a patient's point of view.) ibid. *1,* 307–8

1981

Parish, G. 'Faulty Fibres?' *Nursing Mirror,* October, p. 41

Ramsey, A. M. 'Myalgic Encephalomyelitis: A Baffling Syndrome.' ibid. October, p. 41

1983

Behan, P. O., Fegan, K. G., and Bell, E. J. 'Myalgic Encephalomyelitis—Report of an Epidemic.' *Journal of the Royal College of General Practitioners*, June, p. 335
Bell, E., Irvine, K., Gardiner, A. and Rodger, J. 'Coxsackie B Infection in a General Medical Unit.' *Scottish Medical Journal, 28*, 157
Keighley, B. D. and Bell, E. J. 'Sporadic Myalgic Encephalomyelitis in a Rural Practice.' *Journal of the Royal College of General Practitioners*, June, p. 339

1984

Arnold, D., Bore, P., Radda, G., Styles, P. and Taylor, D. 'Excessive Intracellular Acidosis of Skeletal Muscle on Exercise in a Patient with a Post-viral Exhaustion/Fatigue Syndrome.' *The Lancet, i*, 1367
Bell, E. J. and McCartney, R. 'A Study of Coxsackie B Virus Infections, 1972/1983.' *Journal of Hygiene (Cambridge), 93*, 197
Calder, B. D. and Warnock, P. J. 'Coxsackie B Infection in a Scottish General Practice.' *General Practitioner Journal*, January
Gray, J. A. 'Some Long-term Sequelae of Coxsackie B Virus Infection.' *General Practitioner Journal*, January
Murdoch, J. C. 'M. E. and the General Practitioner.' *New Zealand Family Practitioner, 11*, 127
Smith, D. 'Royal Free Disease May be Viral!' *General Practitioner*, January
—— 'Royal Free Disease is Not All in the Mind'. *New Scientist*, January, p. 20
Tsukada, N., Behan, W. and Behan, P. 'Search for Autoantibodies to Endothelial and Smooth Muscle Cells in Patients with MS.' *Acta Neuropathologica (Berlin), 66*, 134

1985

*Behan, P. O., Behan, W. M. H. and Bell, E. J. 'The Postviral Fatigue Syndrome — An Analysis of Findings in 50 Cases'. *Journal of Infection, 10*, 211
——, Koh, Ch-S., Yanagisawa, N., Taketomi, T. and Tsukada, N. 'Peripheral Nervous Tissue Injury Induced by Galactocerebroside and Galactocerebroside Immune Complexes.' *Acta Neuropathologica (Berlin), 66*, 274
Byrne, E., Trounce, I. and Bennett, X. 'Chronic Relapsing Myalgia (?Post-viral): Clinical, Histological and Biochemical Studies.' *Australian and New Zealand Medical Journal*, 15
*Jamal, G. A. and Hansen, S. 'Electrophysiological Studies in the Post-viral Fatigue Syndrome.' *Journal of Neurology, Neurosurgery and Psychiatry, 48*, 691
Rowlandson, P. H. and Stephens, J. A. 'Maturation of Cutaneous Reflex Responses Recorded in the Lower Limb of Man'. *Development Medicine and Child Neurology, 27*, 425

1988

*Behan, P. O. and Behan, M. W. 'Postviral Fatigue Syndrome.' *Crit. Rev. Neurobiol., 4* (2)
*Dowsett, E. G. 'Human enteroviral infection.' *J. Hosp. Infect., 11*, 103–15
Ramsay, M. *'Myalgic Encephalomyelitis and Post Viral Fatigue States. The Saga of Royal Free Disease,'* Section edition, Gower Medical Publishing

INDEX

abdominal emergency, acute 38
acetylcholine 45
Adelaide (Australia) outbreak
    (1949–51) 9, 26
adenoviruses 30
    type 3 27
    type 5 27
adrenaline 45
Alaska epidemic (1954) 9
allergy 31
ankylosing spondylitis 48
antibodies 22, 23
anti-depressants 41
antigens 22, 24
    alteration by virus infection 48–9
    blood tests 33
    HLA 48
    skin tests 33
appendicitis, acute 38
arboviruses 30
arthropathies 32
asthma 31, 32
atopy 31
Ayrshire (UK) outbreak (1980–1) 27

B cells (lymphocytes) 23
Bethesda (USA) epidemic (1953) 9
blood tests 36
Bornholm 29
Buclofen 44

carcinoid 49
chemical allergy, post-viral infection
    32
chickenpox virus 49
clinical presentation 15–21
    acute 15–16
    alternating depression/cheerfulness
        15, 16
    arthritis 48
    bad taste in mouth 15
    clumsiness 15
    coldness of extremities 15
    collapse 15
    concentration difficulty 16
    conjunctivitis 15
    delusions of persecution 38
    depression 15, 16

diarrhoea 15
dizziness 19
drug sensitivity 43
fatigue 40
feeling awful 16
feeling of weakness/illness 14
fever 15
gastric upsets 41
giddiness 15
gynaecological disorder 48
headache 15
hypoglycaemia 46
hypothermia 15
insomnia 15, 16
liver enlargement 15
loss of appetite 14
loss of memory 16
lymph node enlargement 15
malabsorption 47
muscle tenderness 15
muscle twitching 15
nightmares 16
noises in ears 15
numbness 15
nystagmus (flickering of eyes) 15
pain 19
pallor 15
palpitations 15
personality disorder 38
pins and needles 15
premenstrual 45
recovery 15
relapses 16
shivering attacks 15
sleeping difficulties 15
sore throat 15
steatorrhoea 48
stiffness of neck 15
tiredness 16
variation of symptoms from day to
    day 16
vomiting 15
coeliac disease 37, 47
    schizophrenia associated 47
colitis 32
complement system 23
coronary thrombosis 38
cortisone 45–6

149